AN A-Z GIRLS GUIDE TO CREATING A LIFE YOU LOVE

TIFFANY NICOLE

Printed in the United States of America

An imprint of Tiffany Nicole Global
PMB 110
1750 Powder Springs Road, Suite 190
Marietta, GA 30064-4861
www.tiffanynicoleglobal.com

ISBN: 978-1-7342684-6-1

Ordering Information:

Quantity sales. Special discounts are available on quantity purchases by corporations, associations, and others. For details, contact the publisher at the address above.

Orders by U.S. trade bookstores and wholesalers. Please contact Tiffany Nicole Global: Tel: (404) 312-4102; or visit www.tiffanynicoleglobal.com.

ACKNOWLEDGMENTS

This book came about because of my heartfelt desire to see young women win all over the world. I am so fulfilled when I can talk to and pour into them to help them understand who they are and why they are here. Living life on purpose is at the forefront of my mind every day, and writing this book was a very important part of my purpose; however, I wouldn't have been able to do it without a few people in my corner.

Most of all, I'd like to thank God. He is my Heavenly Father, my best friend, and I would be nothing without Him. He was with me throughout the entire journey to completing this project. He stayed up with me at night and woke me up feeling refreshed every morning. He helped me put every word on every page and lifted my head when I felt like giving up. I dedicate this book to Him and give Him all the glory for my life, my purpose, my health, my strength, and my blessings.

Next, I want to thank my family, who supports me so consistently. Even though I live far away from everyone I know, talking to y'all on Facetime and texting you throughout the day made me feel closer. You read chapters, listened to me, made me laugh, and prayed for and encouraged me. Some of you even visited me. Thank you, Papa, Mommy, Tracy, Tamara, Joy, Uncle Tyuan, and Tonja.

A special shout out goes to Patty, who is not just my aunt but my friend, my big sister, and another mother. You inspire me as a writer, a prayer warrior, and a woman of God. I love you so much for your support, love, and wisdom not just throughout this process but throughout my entire life.

Thank you to my inspirations, my nieces and nephews. You all bring me so much joy and treat your Auntie like a she-ro! Everything I do is to prove you can dream big and accomplish anything you set your mind to. I love you, Terrance, Keenan, Alyiah, Tyson, Anya, and Ari. *"Y'all can have anything y'all want."* *inside joke*

Thanks to my *fr-amily*, my godbrother GoGo, my bestie Kim, and "Mama B" who checked on me when I locked myself in the house on the computer for days on end, traveled out of the country by myself to write and was only getting a few hours of sleep every night. Thanks for being there through this marathon and helping me reach the finish line. I love y'all with my whole heart.

And last but certainly not least, thanks to the team of fierce women who helped me put this project together. You guided me through all the hills and valleys with your wisdom, expertise, and hard work. This group includes my editor Cynthia Tucker; my graphic designers Ana Tomic and Tayyaba Bano; my PR manager Jasmine Murray of Milan360 Strategies; image consultant Sharice Styles of Powerhouse Style Club; and my amazing photographer Kimberly Taylor of Kimazing Photography! Thank you, beautiful ladies, for being the wind beneath the wings of this project.

DEDICATION

This book is dedicated to Betty F. Massey—my grandmother and my Queen. You taught me that with a close relationship with Jesus, prayer, a loving heart, and a dedication to family, my crown will never come off. You were my best friend and I miss you every day. I will always live to make you proud.

TABLE OF CONTENTS

INTRO

Girls today have so many issues coming at them from every angle, even more than I did growing up. In my work as a coach and minister to girls ages 12–21, I've heard it all. Between pressure from social media, peers, and parents, girls battle with temptations for sex, drugs, and alcohol and deal with low self-esteem, depression, and feelings of worthlessness. It takes time for them to learn who they are and how to push past those problems and into their destiny. In this book, I explore these issues and give girls practical tools to relieve the pressure, dodge the above issues, and put on their crowns to become Queens.

I wish I could tell you I always conducted myself as a Queen. I wish I could tell you that I always knew I was royalty and treated myself with love, self-worth, care, and respect. I wish I could even tell you that I have always liked myself, but the truth is there were times when I couldn't find one good thing about myself in the mirror and felt like I did not want or deserve to be here. I remember putting on a fake smile for friends and family pretending I didn't think my life was a total waste and that being born was the biggest mistake ever. I was lost, confused, and weighed down by low self-esteem.

It isn't like I grew up in foster care or had to duck and dodge bullets. I grew up in a normal two-parent home in a decent neighborhood with two sisters and a brother and then, later, a cousin. My grandparents were in my life and I was raised in the church and had fun with my friends. I watched my favorite shows and sang my heart out to 90s music, got good grades, and ate three meals a day. I was grateful for what I had, but none of those things taught me how to love myself, what my worth was, and what I should and should not put up with in life. I didn't even know any of those things mattered. My parents were great, but I don't think most parents know how to teach their daughters these things—even if they do, they don't have the time between work, raising children, and trying to run a household. We spent countless hours a week in church, but I was just there—it wasn't in me yet. When you don't know who you are, why you are, and what you're worth, you'll be roaming around clueless about life, relationships, and may end up looking for validation in all the wrong places and faces.

One of my favorite quotes is by the late, great Myles Munroe, who once said, "*When purpose is not known, abuse is inevitable.*" Inevitable means certain to happen. When I first read this quote, it didn't really sink in until I realized one day that I didn't know my own purpose and I was literally abusing myself with bad choices, the wrong crowd, too much partying, relationships with awful guys who didn't care about me, and was literally putting myself down every day. Yes, I had a good job, a few friends, and a tight-knit family, but I was sinking slowly in my own feelings about myself because I didn't know my purpose and I definitely didn't know my worth.

So on top of not knowing why God made me, I had an overcrowded mouth full of teeth, acne, a big forehead that I hadn't learned yet how to embrace, and a body I didn't know how to celebrate. It wasn't until I actually gave my life to Christ, learned to seek Him for my purpose, and asked Him to show me my worth that I started living with intention instead of further abusing myself. I learned that He made me to be a great and strong woman of God and to be an example to girls just like you so you can avoid a lot of confusion, pain, heartache, and low self-esteem and take charge of your life. It is my prayer that the words in this book inspire, encourage, and motivate you to make choices now that will pay off later in order to have the good life you were created to live.

This book goes from A–Z, breaking down the exact principles I have applied, and still do apply, in my life. It wasn't easy, but it was worth it. A young woman of worth and purpose is a Queen in the making. I want you to know the things I wish I knew at your age—walk in them now and begin to find, follow, flow, and fulfill your God-given right to a royal life. It definitely won't be perfect but, prayerfully, this book will give you the foundation and the ability to overcome obstacles and live not just your best life but your *blessed* life.

AUTHENTICITY

Therefore be imitators of God as beloved children. Walk in love, as Christ loved us and gave Himself for us as a fragrant offering and a sacrifice to God. (Ephesians 5:1-2)

*A*uthenticity is one of the most important values you can have to live a truly fulfilling life. To be authentic means to be real, transparent, and genuine in your daily actions with everyone. Young girls are usually told to sit still, be quiet, and act like a lady. I have always been outspoken, so when I grew up and asked questions, I was told I was talking back or being disrespectful. By the time I was a teen, I was taught that speaking up for myself was wrong. I either had to shut up and pretend I was cool with what was going on or risk saying what was on my mind and getting punished or slapped in the face. Are you so busy trying to be who your parents, teachers, pastors, and friends want you to be—from toddler to teen—that by the time you are grown, you don't even know who you are at all?

REJECTION CAN SHAPE US

Sometimes rejection can cause you to be uncomfortable being real. For instance, I loved being in the gospel choir in the ninth grade. I grew up in church and loved to sing (even though I wasn't the strongest singer, but you couldn't tell me that), and it was a place where I could be myself, have fun, and express myself through my love of music. A guy there teased me every chance he got. He talked about my teeth with braces, my girly clothes, and how I wasn't as pretty as the friends he'd see me with at the mall over the weekend. He would say these things out loud in front of people! I got so tired of his insults that the following year, I refused to join the gospel choir! The humiliation of being bullied directly affected my choices in school, changed how I saw myself, and made me feel like I couldn't be me. This is not the way God wants you to live.

REAL IS NOT RUDE

Now being authentic does not mean being rude or ratchet or tacky. It doesn't mean saying whatever comes to your mind and walking around purposely hurting people's feelings and causing them to feel uncomfortable being themselves. No way. I know doing this gets you more likes and clicks on social media while people call you "real," but the truth is, it's *real* rude, *real* tacky, and *real* nasty. You won't get anywhere meaningful in life being a bully, and putting others down will stop your blessings.

WHAT IS AUTHENTICITY?

Authenticity means being true to who you are and making sure your choices, actions, and words line up with your values, personality, and beliefs. But what if you are a bad person and have no values or beliefs? Then being real to who you believe you should be isn't the best thing to strive for. Authenticity is about loving yourself, being real with yourself about the areas in which you have room to grow, and doing the hard work to become better every day.

If you aren't a very social person and don't like large crowds, why continue agreeing to attend events that make you miserable? If you like listening to a certain type of music, why pretend you don't like it as soon as someone teases you about it? Forcing yourself to do things that don't make you happy will cause bitterness to build up in your heart. There are a lot of people walking around miserable because they aren't walking in their truth. So be free, be happy, be authentic, and speak up when you are asked to do things that contradict who you are.

WHO ARE YOU?

The first step to being 100% authentic is to get to know yourself. You can't possibly be true to who you are if you don't even know who you are. Many girls spend most of their time watching others on social media and television and trying to portray the personalities and characteristics they see. You may look at the way celebrities or influencers dress and think you have to look like them. You see a commercial or TV show and automatically try to measure up. You use their slang to sound cool even though it doesn't even feel right or natural. You have to figure out what you like so the only person you look at as "goals" is yourself. Authenticity is about knowing yourself, doing what makes you feel comfortable, and flowing in your own awesomeness.

When I moved to Chicago, everyone said I had a strong East Coast accent. I didn't hear it, but I definitely wasn't going to try to sound like them because I grew up in a different part of the country.

On social media, you see lots of filtered faces full of makeup posing sexily for the camera, selling tummy tea and waist trainers to try to be sex symbols so they can get likes and feel accepted. Then you practice certain poses and angles in the mirror. Little do you know, some of those people had thousands of dollars of surgery on their faces and bodies to get all of those followers and likes. Why even try to be like a girl who isn't being herself? It is so exhausting trying to keep up with people who are trying to keep up with other people. That is a race nobody can win.

The only person you should try to be like is who God created you to be. You are enough . . . without a filter, without a script, and without a camera. The Greek word for hypocrite means actor. Your life is not a movie. You can't cut a scene out, edit the moments, or have rehearsals and rewrites. Your life is real and you only get one shot. Learn who you are and what makes you happy so you can live the rest of your life as who you are meant to be and not someone you are pretending to be.

LEARNING WHO YOU ARE

Do you know what makes you happy? Do you know what motivates you? Do you know your personality type? Do you know your real favorite color and not just the one your best friend likes? Do you know your favorite foods, not just the ones your mama cooks every week? Are you a people person or do you like to spend most of your time alone? Do you want children? Do you like children? What are your biggest fears? All of these things help shape who you are, how you see things, and how you act.

Take a minute to write down all of your likes on one side of the page and dislikes on the other. Then write the things you have done before that you don't like. Once you gain a clearer picture of who you are, what you like, and what you value, you'll be closer to being yourself at all times, even under pressure.

The fear of human opinion disables; trusting in God protects you from that. (Proverbs 29:25)

WHO CARES WHAT THEY THINK?

The second step to living a life of authenticity is to stop living in fear of what people think of you. You must get to a point in life where you are comfortable in your own skin and love who you are inside and out. Of course, you aren't perfect. No one is. You may have some character flaws that you want to get rid of. You may have some bad habits that you'd like to break. You may even have some physical flaws you want to improve; however, these imperfections shouldn't stop you from living fearlessly and divorcing yourself from the opinions of other imperfect humans. They can't do anything to you but talk, and talk is cheap. Yes, words hurt, but they should never make you change who you are, especially because those people have their own set of issues. I've heard before that when someone points a finger, there are three pointing back at them. Why trip over what someone says about you when they have a boatload of flaws of their own? When you are being yourself, you will eventually attract the right people in your life.

WHAT'S GOOD?

Your next assignment is to write down every single good thing about yourself even if you've never shown that side on a regular basis. If you can sing and nobody knows, write it down. If you are funny, write it down. If you are good at math, have a compassionate heart, or a great sense of style, write it down. Ask those closest to you to describe the positive things about you and your personality and write those things down as well.

FORGET THEM

I used to think my ex-boyfriend thought everything about me was great. He would compliment me and make me feel loved and admired. He called me smart and fun and sweet. This drew me in and made me put my guard down. I was my total self around him and his family. When he saw how confident I was, little by little, he tried to change me and make me feel less sure of myself. He once whispered in my ear, "Jeez, your hair gets nappy after you hit the water. You were cute when we came into the water park, but now you look a mess compared to everyone else."

When I wouldn't agree with him about something, he escalated his verbal abuse by calling me names and trying to make me feel like I was crazy or stupid. I was in my 20s with a great job, own condo, and car. I was doing great, but slowly but surely, the self-esteem I took years building in high school started crumbling. We went to the same church and also worked together, so at first, I chalked it up to his stress level or the fact that we were always together and were just getting on each other's nerves. But after the emotional abuse became physical, I could no longer make excuses for him.

We were high school sweethearts who reunited after college, and the man I thought I would one day marry became the man of my nightmares. In the middle of premarital counseling, I ended the relationship. I could no longer pretend to everyone around me that we were a perfect couple, and I definitely could no longer look in the mirror at myself every day knowing my life had become a lie. I could no longer fake smile at work or church when deep down I knew I would be in tears behind closed doors. I knew that God did not want me to suffer like I was and that I deserved better, so I walked away.

I wish I could say that when I freed myself of that toxic relationship, I instantly felt beautiful, happy, and whole again. It took time to learn who I was and what made me feel like myself. Authenticity is a journey. I had to take the steps above and renew my mind so I could live a life free of what others thought and stop dwelling on what other damaged souls said about me.

True friends and loved ones will never make you feel like you have to pretend and hide your true feelings and personality. They will push you to be true to who you are, they will celebrate what makes you special, and they will lovingly encourage you to be the best YOU that you can be. If you are or have been in a bad relationship or friendship that causes you to question who you are and every decision is based on someone else's opinion, free yourself, get support from real friends or family, and take the time to heal from the damage that was done.

> **Am I saying this now to win the approval of people or God? Am I trying to please people? If I were still trying to please people, I would not be Christ's servant. (Galatians 1:10)**

STOP COMPROMISING

The final step to building and maintaining an authentic life is to stop doing things that don't benefit who you are and start doing things that motivate you to be yourself. You cannot live a fulfilled and real life by being a programmed robot just to fit in or be someone else's version of amazing. Be your own version of amazing. You can work every day to become better, but don't try to be like someone else. You are enough just the way you were created. You don't have to follow the same path as someone else just to feel like you belong. That path may have worked for them, but God has a specific plan for you. The more you seek Him and read His Word about who you are, the clearer the picture will become about the things you were created to do. You are no good to yourself, your family, or to God if you are trying to walk anyone else's path but your own.

For example, I've never been shy even among strangers. Most people aren't used to my level of confidence when they meet me. I have a strong personality. People love me or hate me. I've been told that I make people feel small or insecure. They say, "You're a nice person, but you're just a little too much." Being told this over and over growing up caused me to dim my light to fit in. For some reason, I always seemed to attract quiet and laid-back people, and I wondered why I had to be the most cheerful in the group. My own so-called friends liked being around me for what seemed like "entertainment," but my confidence even when I had a bad day made them feel some type of way. Things would start off great and then they'd say, "How are you always so happy? I wish I could be like that." I didn't even think that was a bad thing. Most times when a friend or loved one is comparing who you are to who they are, they see something in you they wish they had. Watch out for red flags! When someone gives you compliments and puts a but at the end or have something negative to say after, they may secretly be jealous.

People didn't realize that I struggled with acceptance too and that I wasn't always confident. They didn't realize how hard I worked to finally get to a place where I was comfortable being nobody else but Tiffany Nicole. They didn't see how many versions of myself I went through to finally find the one that was custom made for me. They only saw the result of my hard work on myself and started hating. Eventually, their insecurities would appear, and those people would disappear from my life. And I thank God for exposing and removing them. Don't mourn anyone's absence who didn't make you feel like your presence was a present.

When you continue to learn more about yourself, who you are will start screaming so loud on the inside that you can't ignore her. You can try to be a watered-down version of yourself and be miserable or allow the real you to come out and shine and be rewarded with a meaningful, happy life.

BE GENUINE

The last way to be authentic is to genuinely show concern and care for others. When you ask someone, "How are you?" being authentic means you actually care about how they are doing. If you know they were going through a hard time recently, check up on them and offer a helping hand if you are led to do so. When you give a compliment, meaning what you say is important. If you are only saying things to make conversation, you'll come off as manipulative, like you are trying to get something from them. If someone is sick or sad and asks you to pray for them, being authentic means you will actually pray for them and not just say you will or leave the praying hands emoji in their comments or on a text. Make sure to follow up and ask them if things have gotten better. Be sincere anytime you are reaching out to people. This world has enough fakes.

I have worked hard to have authenticity in my life. I didn't know how important it was until I was in my 20s, when, at one point, I couldn't even recognize myself. I dressed different, did my hair different, and even spoke different based on an image I thought I should portray. Pretty soon, my heart was hardened from the pain of not being myself. I had to start from scratch and ask God to forgive me for trying to be someone other than who I was made to be. He started showing me why He created me the way He did and how He saw me, and I was shocked at how off track I was. His love led the way to me becoming who I am today, and He will do the same for you if you let Him.

PRAYER

Father, in the name of Jesus, thank you for creating me to be unique. I know that you do all things well. You said that I am fearfully and wonderfully made, and I love that you took your time and put certain gifts, talents, and characteristics in me for a reason. Forgive me for not seeing how special I am all the time. I know you created me for a purpose, and I want to live an authentic life so I can fulfill that purpose and be genuine in all that I do. Help me ignore the negative things people say about me when I am being my true self. I rebuke any bad things they have said or that I have said about myself. Surround me with people who love me and make me feel comfortable being 100% me. Thank you for setting me free from their opinions and for causing me every day to see myself how you see me in Jesus' name. Amen!

B R A V E R Y

Fight the good fight of faith, lay hold on eternal life, whereunto thou art also called, and hast professed a good profession before many witnesses. (1 Timothy 6:12)

ravery is defined as courageous behavior or character. To be brave means that you will charge ahead in life no matter the circumstances. Life is a battle, but the Bible tells us to fight the good fight of faith. It is called a good fight because, through Jesus, you have the victory and can always win with Him on your side. You cannot control people, their actions, or the things that happen to you, but you can control your response by choosing bravery. There are several steps you can take to make sure you stay brave at all times.

〰〰〰〰〰〰〰〰〰〰〰〰〰〰〰〰〰〰〰〰〰〰〰〰〰〰〰〰〰〰〰〰〰〰

Rejoice always, pray without ceasing, give thanks in all circumstances; for this is the will of God in Christ Jesus for you. (1 Thessalonians 5:16-18)

〰〰〰〰〰〰〰〰〰〰〰〰〰〰〰〰〰〰〰〰〰〰〰〰〰〰〰〰〰〰〰〰〰〰

START YOUR DAY WITH JESUS

It is important to cover your day in prayer when you first get up in the morning. After making your bed (you do that right?), start thanking God for waking you up and giving you life, health, and strength and anything else you are grateful for. Then pray for peace, joy, and protection to cover your day. Thank God for giving you the wisdom to overcome any issue and ask Him to send angels before you to make sure things go smoothly. If you have important tasks or decisions to make that day, ask Him for grace to complete everything without stress, strain, or struggle.

When you pray and put your day in the hands of God, you can face the day with a lighter load, knowing He is in control and is walking with you hand in hand every step of the way. The Bible says to pray without ceasing. Throughout the day, you can talk to Him and know that He is right there. This will give you bravery all day long because you aren't in this by yourself.

I find that when I am in a rush or get distracted and don't cover my day, I am a mess. I forget things, I lose track of time, I'm like that Snickers commercial when people are hangry. I'm irritated and I am not my best self. I learned a long time ago that waking up early to be with God makes the whole day brighter and better. It is a privilege to be able to start your day by sitting at His feet, talking to Him about anything on your mind, and hearing from Him so you can stand solid and not fold at the slightest thing. Anytime you feel the opposite of brave, pray again.

God will never get tired of you coming to Him. He wants to be a part of your day.

> **Those who guard their mouths and their tongues keep themselves from calamity. (Proverbs 21:23)**

SPEAK POSITIVELY

Watch your words. Be careful what you say against yourself, your life, and your loved ones. If you have a test to take that day and you don't feel prepared, instead of saying, "I know I'm going to fail this test," study harder and say, "I got this. *I can do all things through Christ who gives me strength*" (*Philippians 4:13*). *The memory of the righteous is blessed!*" (*Proverbs 10:7*). Our tongues are very powerful. The Bible calls them pens. You can literally write out your future with the words you speak. If you say it and believe it, that is what you will see. Only speak positive things over yourself so that when you go out in the world, you can face it with bravery because you spoke only the things you wanted to see. Positive faith confessions also work to keep you encouraged. Repeat the following to build yourself up: I am strong. I am wise. I am more than a conqueror. I can handle whatever comes my way. I am resilient. I am blessed. I can tackle any issue. I am healthy. I am loved. I am fearless. I am BRAVE!

SPEAK UP

A trusted friend or family member can help you work through your emotions, encourage you through a storm, and help get your mind off a bad situation by making you laugh or just being there to listen. Only talk to others you know are also living brave lives or can help you work through it—people who won't judge you for being afraid or anxious, people who won't tell your business to others. Tell only those who can motivate you to be brave and overcome your fears.

Don't tell anyone who seems like a magnet for drama. They will add more stress and cause you to doubt yourself even more. If you tell someone messy, you've given them bullets to shoot off at the mouth to someone who won't pray for you but will spread your business. That is the last thing you want.

> *Don't be afraid, I've redeemed you. I've called your name. You're mine. When you're in over your head, I'll be there with you. When you're in rough waters, you will not go down. When you're between a rock and a hard place, it won't be a dead-end—Because I am God, your personal God. (Isaiah 43:1-4)*

TURN FEAR INTO FAITH

God cares about every single detail in your life, and He is with you all the time. When you understand that and know you can call on Him any time, it can stop fear in its tracks. The Bible says "fear not" at least 80 times because God knows everyone has to deal with and conquer fear. He wouldn't tell us not to fear if it was impossible. You can get past any type of fear and live freely.

I remember when I was in a horrible car accident. Someone ran a stop sign and hit me on the driver's side, and my SUV spun around, jumped the curb, and hit a pole. I blacked out and had no idea what day it was and where I was when I woke up. I was in shock. I had no broken bones but was sore for months. I didn't even want to get in a car for a while. I took a Lyft and got rides where I needed to go. Four months later, I finished physical therapy and moved to Atlanta. When I bought a new SUV and started driving again, fear would try to creep in and make me nervous at every stop sign or light. I had to pray, remind myself that God was with me, and turn that fear into faith.

> **When I am afraid, I put my trust in you. In God, whose word I praise—in God I trust and am not afraid. What can mere mortals do to me? (Psalms 56:3-4)**

TRY SOMETHING NEW

Brave people do not let the thought of something new or different scare them off. I remember my first time speaking in public to 500 people. Girl, I was nervous. I am not even a shy person but just the thought of being open up there with everyone watching and hanging on to my every word scared me so bad. So I prepared. I wrote my notes. I practiced. I prayed. I prepared some more, and by the time I got up there, I was so excited to share what God gave me to say. If I had focused on the fact that I had never done anything like that before or accepted the thought of being rejected, I would have gotten stuck and never been able to start the journey to fulfilling my purpose. You have to step out of your comfort zone to see something new and wonderful happen in your life. The more new things you try that stretch you, the less anxiety you will feel each time and open yourself up to amazing possibilities. Another thing I have noticed in my life is that once you conquer one fear, an opportunity to conquer an even bigger one will come up. Will you take the opportunity or make an excuse?

BRAVERY LIST

Write down everything that scares you—not things like spiders and snakes, because I think most girls are uncomfortable around those things and wouldn't willingly jump into a pit with them. I want you to write down the things you have a desire to do but say you never will because of fear, such as "ride a rollercoaster" or "hike up a waterfall" or "speak to a crowd." We will call it the Bravery list.

Once you finish your bravery list, pray over it and ask God for the opportunity to conquer these fears. Then write a date when you'd like to do these things. I call it the "Do Date." It can be a certain age or a certain month and year. Every chance you get, check off the things on your list one by one.

I love to travel, and one of my favorite places to visit is Montego Bay, Jamaica. The last time I went, I went to Dunns River Falls, a waterfall with huge, slippery rocks. It is 600 feet high, and thousands of people visit every day. You have to wear water shoes that have a grip at the bottom because the rocks are huge and slippery. I slipped within five minutes, and my friend got it on camera! I wasn't embarrassed, but I started to doubt if I could make it to the top.

When we walked up, we were in a group of about 15 people. The guide told us to hold hands with the person in front of us and behind us so we could help each other. I went slowly as I watched the girl's footsteps in front of me. At one point, we had to go under a bridge! Picture it—trying to step carefully under a low bridge on top of huge rocks with strong flowing water going in the opposite direction! The first step I took under the bridge, I didn't squat low enough and bumped my head, and my sunglasses slipped and fell down the water. There was an exit about halfway up and I wanted to take it so bad, but I couldn't let myself down. This was on my list of things to conquer, and I was determined to check it off. When I finally made it to the top, I was so relieved. Now I can be honest and say I never want to do it again, but the thrill of knowing that no matter how challenging the task, I can push past the fear and the pain to the finish line makes me feel like I can do anything.

NEVER GIVE UP

Brave people know that everything does not always go as planned. The difference between brave people and everyone else is that brave people never give up. You have to get back up when you fall. You have to shake off the bad thoughts when you are trying something new like I did on the waterfall. I laughed it off and kept it moving.

Whether you have to present a project, start a new school, end a friendship or relationship, face someone who talked behind your back, or admit to making a mistake, do it with bravery and fearlessness, knowing you can overcome it and come out a winner regardless of what it looks like right now.

PRAY SOME MORE

Whenever you need an extra boost of bravery, say this prayer:

Father, in the name of Jesus, thank you for doing the hardest thing ever known to man by dying on the cross for me. Because you conquered death, I am more than a conqueror through you! You gave me the victory over anything I put my mind to do. You placed in me your spirit that causes me to win over and over again. I can't lose with you by my side, and I thank you for making me brave in the face of fear, danger, sickness, or any situation. I am brave. I am strong, and NOTHING will overtake me in Jesus' name. Amen.

CONFIDENCE

But blessed is the one who trusts in the Lord, whose confidence is in Him. (Jeremiah 17:7)

onfidence is the feeling or belief that you can count on someone or something. Some people put their trust in money. They are obsessed with the commas in their bank account balance; they invest in the stock market; and if those things were to crash, they would be lost. Some people put their confidence in what they own, like their houses, cars, and designer clothes. They show off and brag and feel like as long as they have those things, they have all they need. What if those things were taken away? Would they feel worthless? The only One you can truly trust and believe in is God. He loves you so much, will never let you down, and stays the same day after day.

GOD CREATED US TO BE GREAT

"For I know the plans I have for you," declares the LORD, "plans to prosper you and not to harm you, plans to give you hope and a future." (Jeremiah 29:11)

Confidence is knowing without a doubt that God has your back and that everything you need has already been placed inside of you. You can be confident that God wants you to win in every area of your life. He wants you to win at school, home, in your relationships, your career, and even your hobbies. He made you to be a winner. When you don't know how much you mean to God and the truth that He wants you to prosper, your confidence will remain low. The more you learn about God's love for you and His plans for you, the more your confidence will grow.

TRUE CONFIDENCE COMES FROM TRUSTING IN GOD

But blessed is the man who trusts me, God, the woman who sticks with God. They're like trees replanted in Eden, putting down roots near the rivers. Never a worry through the hottest of summers, never dropping a leaf. Serene and calm through droughts, bearing fresh fruit every season. (Jeremiah 17:7-8)

Picture yourself as a tree planted in a beautiful garden. Now picture it being 115 degrees with no breeze, but you don't break a sweat. Picture haters walking by with something to say, people gossiping, parents misunderstanding you, and fake friends doing you dirty, but you can't be shaken. Picture yourself every year still growing and glowing. When you rely on God, He will put the right people in your life to help you along the way, and the plan He has for you will come together slowly but surely. It doesn't mean things will be perfect all the time, but you can trust that everything will work out for your good because God is right there with you. That is where your confidence comes from. You can trust God to keep you cool in heated confrontations, strong in tough situations, and joyful in sad times.

CONFIDENCE VS. SELF-CONFIDENCE

There is a difference between confidence and self-confidence, but they both work together. Self-confidence is believing in yourself and your abilities and being courageous, bold, and positive in what you can do. To have self-confidence, you must know that what makes you who you are was purposely put inside of you to succeed. You were not born just so people can say, "Oh, she's so cute! She looks just like her mama . . . or she has her daddy's eyes!" God actually placed special talents, abilities, and skills in you that will honor Him and bless the people you encounter. Every single thing about you is designed to help you make an impact on the world! People are looking for what YOU have to offer. When you know that, something will click, you'll realize how powerful you are with God working through you, and you will stop comparing yourself to others. You will also stop picking at each and every flaw you think you have. Then you can walk boldly on the right path to being, doing, and having everything God created you to be, do, and have!

I can do all things through Christ who strengthens me (Philippians 4:13)

WALK IN CONFIDENCE NO MATTER WHAT

You can learn a lot about keeping your head up and being confident even when being put down from a beautiful girl named Kheris Rogers. Throughout elementary school, she was bullied for her dark skin. She was attending a mostly white school in Los Angeles and was the darkest of four other black children. At 11 years old, she was asked to draw a picture of herself, and the teacher gave her a black crayon. The bullies made her feel so bad that she asked to stay in the bathtub longer because she thought it would lighten her skin. She would come home crying and very upset.

Even when Kheris' mother switched her to a more diverse school, she was still bullied by black children for her darker complexion. Kheris' grandmother would encourage her and her sister to feel beautiful in their skin and told them they were "flexin' in their complexion." One day, her older sister, Taylor Pollard, posted a photo of Kheris and used the hashtag #FlexinInTheirComplexion. The tweet went viral, and they launched their own clothing line in April 2017.

Instead of allowing her bullies to win, Kheris responded to the racism and colorism with confidence and creativity and sold over $200,000 in t-shirts at 10 years old. A year later, she has gotten the attention of celebrities like Snoop Dogg, Alicia Keys, and Steve Harvey. Kheris was even featured in a Nike ad campaign. Now she's as confident as ever, and Flexin' in My Complexion is proof that when you ignore what anyone has to say about you and walk in confidence, you can drown out the negativity and overcome bullying.

> ***Your beauty should not come from outward adornment, such as elaborate hairstyles and the wearing of gold jewelry or fine clothes. Rather, it should be that of your inner self, the unfading beauty of a gentle and quiet spirit, which is of great worth in God's sight. (1 Peter 3:3-4)***

EMBRACING YOUR UNIQUE BEAUTY

When most people hear the word beauty, they automatically think of what is on the outside because that is what you are taught online and on television. God wants you to think about developing what is inside of you, which is far more valuable. Everyone's definition of beauty is different. Television, magazines, and social media share their own images of what beauty is, but God's definition of beauty is different.

Your favorite celebrities weren't always super glamorous. Cardi B wore her hair in cornrows and had to wait until she "got a bag and fixed her teeth," but she was confident on Instagram way before her record deal. Rihanna wore her hair in a natural afro before she was discovered for her singing talent in Barbados and now has her own makeup and clothing line. Winne Harlow was picked out of thousands of women even though she has a skin condition that others teased her for, and now she's modeling for all the top designers like Versace, Chanel, and Gucci. So many of the celebrities you know and love tapped into their inner beauty, creative ideas, and personalities long before they were known for their outer beauty.

You can do the same by focusing on your talents, skills, abilities, and attitude. Develop those attributes and nobody can stop you. If you are a great singer or dancer, practice as much as possible. If you can draw or create new and exciting designs in fashion, put on fashion shows and ask your friends to support your brand. If you have a great business mind, make it sharper by reading and studying. These are the things that no one can take away from you no matter how you look.

> *But the fruit of the Spirit produces this kind of fruit in our lives: love, joy, peace, patience, kindness, goodness, faithfulness, gentleness, and self-control. (Galatians 5:22-23)*

Of course, you should always be presentable when you leave the house but only paying attention to your face, hair, and body is like painting a house full of junk. The junk in your heart could represent negative thoughts, bad habits, past hurt, and a nasty attitude. The Bible says you should spend most of your time out of the mirror and in God's Word to clean the junk out and replace it with the qualities He finds beautiful, which is found in the fruit of the Spirit. The amplified translation of the Bible says:

> *But the fruit of the Spirit [the result of His presence within us] is love [unselfish concern for others], joy,*

[inner] peace, patience [not the ability to wait, but how we act while waiting], kindness, goodness, faithfulness, gentleness, self-control.

~~~~~~

The fruit of the Spirit is like a breath of fresh air. Imagine yourself in a room full of people who have just rolled in a pile of garbage. Smelly right? Now imagine you walk out of the room and see someone who just rolled in your favorite scent and they give you a hug. It would be refreshing right? That is how it is when you start to spend time developing the fruit of the Spirit. You go from funky to fragrant. These qualities cannot be put on with a makeup brush, a frontal, or even with a new outfit. They must be studied. You do this by praying and reading the Word in order to improve your inside while accepting what is on the outside.

SELF-CONFIDENCE VS. ARROGANCE

There is a difference between self-confidence and arrogance. Self-confidence comes from knowing that what God put in you is enough to achieve your goals. Arrogance comes from pride when you think YOU are the reason great things are happening for you. Arrogance also makes you think you are better than others, and that is not of God. You can be humbled very quickly when you walk in arrogance.

AFFIRMATIONS

Affirmations are short phrases you can speak out loud to build self-confidence. In any area you need confidence in, write what you want to see in that area. Each day when you have a free moment, speak it out loud until you feel more confident. You can write them on sticky notes or index cards or even have your phone remind you each day. Here are the ones I created for myself, and you can say them too:

- ♛ I'm super lit! God's Spirit lives in me. I have no choice but to be poppin'. (Gal. 2:20)
- ♛ I'm a champion! God causes me to triumph, and all I do is win! (2 Cor 2:14)
- ♛ I got the drip! God calls me the salt of the Earth and I add flavor wherever I go. (Matthew 5:13)
- ♛ I'm a princess becoming a Queen! God calls me royalty. (1 Peter 2:9)
- ♛ I'm NOT GUILTY! Jesus bonded me out with His life, the chargers were dropped, and the receipts were deleted. (Romans 3:22)
- ♛ I have authority! Jesus paid the cost for me to be the boss and gave me power. (Romans 3:25)
- ♛ I'm healed! God stripped away the power of sickness and disease, and it can't touch me. (Isaiah 53:55)
- ♛ I'm all the way up! God calls me the head and says I'm above, not beneath. (Deut. 28:12)
- ♛ I'm stamped with approval! God validates me and I don't have to look to others for it. (Psalms 37:6)
- ♛ I'm safe! God's gang of angels protect me wherever I go. (Psalms 91:11)
- ♛ I'm never alone! God is my bestie, and He never leaves me or lets me down! (Deut. 31:16)

♔ I'm loved! God is crazy about me and no lames against me shall prosper! (Rom 8:38-39)

♔ I'm a masterpiece! God made me by hand and prepared an amazing life for me! (Psalms 139:14-16)

♔ I'm unbothered! God fulfills and satisfies me, and evil can't touch me! (Psalms 19:23)

PRAYER

Father, in the name of Jesus, thank you so much for your love and kindness toward me. From this day forward, I promise to accept myself as you created me and not compare myself to anyone else. Forgive me for the times I have put myself down and thinking that beauty is only skin deep. I now know I should work on my inner beauty by seeking you, reading your Word, and striving to walk in the fruit of the Spirit. Help me develop those things so that, wherever I go, people see you. I now can walk in confidence knowing that you love me, knowing that I am enough, and knowing that you created me as I am for a purpose. Amen.

D R E A M

Commit to the Lord whatever you do, and he will establish your plans. (Proverbs 16:3)

I know you've heard it a lot already—Dream big! Chase your dreams! Dreams come true! But you probably haven't grasped how to turn what is in your head and heart to what you see in front of you. Maybe your dreams are jumbled up with the dreams your family and teachers have for you. Or maybe you have given no thought to what you want for yourself. It's okay. No matter where you are in your life, it is never too late to dream and make that dream a reality.

Make is the keyword, meaning to build something out of parts. When God puts a desire in your heart to become or do something and it starts to take over your thoughts, that is when you should take action. It is up to you to not only talk about it but to build it step by step every single day. First, you should pray about it to make sure that what you are dreaming of is actually coming from the right place, not just because

31

you saw someone else do it or heard that it makes a lot of money. The last thing you want to do is to waste time and effort doing something God didn't put in your destiny. I have seen so many people trying to make someone else's dream come true for themselves and end up disappointed when it didn't work because it wasn't meant to be for them.

> ***Suppose one of you wants to build a tower. Won't you first sit down and estimate the cost to see if you have enough money to complete it? (Luke 14:28)***

DO YOUR RESEARCH

When I was young, I used to watch "I Dream of Jeannie." She lived in a bottle and would grant the wishes of the man who found her. He would make a wish and all she had to do was blink and it appeared. One Halloween, my sister picked a "Jeannie" outfit to wear to school. It was funny because it was cold that year in Maryland and she had to wear the two-piece costume with a turtleneck. When she got to school, her best friend had the same costume on! She was so mad! Then, of course, I got on her nerves by trying to get her to grant my wish. The only wish she promised to grant was to punch me in the face!

If you have a dream and don't know what it takes to see it become a reality, then all you have is a wish, and wishes only come true on TV. Since this is real life, you can't find a genie in a bottle to blink and make your dreams happen by snapping your fingers. And you can't wish upon a star like the song says. You actually have to know what it takes to get to the goal. I don't know any successful person who has had a dream and didn't become obsessed with the steps it takes so they could start working on making it happen.

Instead of watching TV for hours on end, wasting time, and not being productive, read a book or watch YouTube or IG TV videos of successful people in the industry you'd like to one day join. Doing these things will give you an advantage so you have a head start over the people who aren't doing anything to research their dream. Some girls tell people their dreams year after year but never research or take any steps, and their dream may sadly never come true.

Another kind of research is to pull up the schedule of classes for a recreation center near you and take any classes that will help you prepare for college, internships, or opening a business. For example, if you are interested in opening a bakery, look up cake baking classes during the summer that will help you learn the tricks and techniques from an already-successful baker. Most people wouldn't think to do these things, but leaders and people who want to be the best at what they do learn that stepping out of your comfort zone is necessary. You can also join a FB group to talk to people in your area who are already doing what you want to do. I'm sure some of them would be happy to answer any questions a young lady like you may have. This would also be a chance for them to give back. There are several ways to learn more about what it takes to attain your dream so you can stop talking about it and start living it.

Then the Lord replied: "Write down the vision and make it plain on tablets so they may run when they read it" (Habakkuk 2:2)

CREATE A PLAN (YOUR GPS)

Once you've done your research, now is the time to create a plan so you can achieve your goal. A plan is a detailed proposal for doing or achieving something. When you want to go somewhere you've never been, you use a GPS. It gives you turn-by-turn directions, telling you when and where to go so you can make it to your destination. A plan does the same for your dreams. It is a GPS that tells you what to do and when to do it for ultimate success.

Have you ever tried to go somewhere without the GPS or any directions? Or if you don't drive yet, maybe you've seen someone else struggle to find a building with no directions. They think they can figure it out on their own. It gets super frustrating to get lost and have to pull over or stop and ask someone for help. It also delays your arrival. So what sense does it make to try to achieve a goal or a dream without a GPS? While the GPS in a car or on your phone stands for **G**lobal **P**ositioning **S**ystem, the GPS you will create to make your dreams a reality stands for **G**oal **P**lanning and **P**urpose **S**ystem. It is a written vision with step-by-step directions to help you along the way. This GPS will keep you motivated, informed, and on the right track. When distractions come up, you refer to your GPS. When you feel overwhelmed, you refer to your GPS.

To create a GPS, you must be very specific. It can be written on a piece of paper or on a computer. Start at the top of your page with the word Destination and underneath a specific sentence that details what the dream is. Your dream is the destination you are using your GPS to get to. Let's say my dream is to start selling scarves. A more specific goal is to write, "I will design and sell custom silk scarves in department stores all over the world in the next five years." This goal is not only specific but complete. If someone asked what your dream is, you could answer who (you), what (selling scarves), where (all over the world in department stores), and when (within five years). These are the key pieces of a Goal Planning and Purpose System (GPS) because it reminds you of the important information you need to get focused on your destination and that God is the one navigating you. He will never lead you wrong.

Since you've already done your research (if you haven't, go back to that section and get started!), you know what it will take and should type the steps in a list. Some of the steps on my list would be:

- Take sewing classes
- Buy sewing machine
- Take fashion and design courses
- Find fabric for scarves
- Create new designs in different color collections
- Get feedback from friends and family and potential customers

This list should be very long. Once you have these typed or written, number them based on order, and place beside it how long it will take. This number is not a deadline but how long it will take to accomplish it. Some things might take 30 minutes, others may take four years (if you are going for a degree or certification or something like that).

Once they are in order, copy and paste each line into an excel spreadsheet or write on a new sheet of paper with spaces underneath to write notes. So the list would look like this:

1	Buy sewing machine	1 hour
2	Take sewing classes	1 year
3	Find fabric for scarves	3 months
4	Create new designs	6 months

This will give you the steps in order and space to write details. For my list, I would put the type of sewing machine I want, how much it is, and where to get it from. If I had to save money for it, I'd write that down too and how I would get that amount of money to buy the machine. Maybe you could get a job, offer babysitting services, or offer to run errands for an elderly person. Once you continue filling in details under each step, you can start to see a roadmap forming. When you use a car or phone GPS, you can push a button to see a map, which shows you where you are and gives you landmarks, signs, lights, and cross streets so you won't miss a turn. This is the same thing with your Goal Purpose and Planning System because once you see this much detail, you can have all of this information in one place.

As you learn more about your dream and the steps it takes to achieve it, you can add more steps and more information for each. You want each step to be in bite-sized goals so you don't get overwhelmed. Writing down "complete a sewing class" can have a bite-sized goal underneath such as "find a sewing class in my area" and then "sign up for a sewing class." Once you start taking those steps, you can start to apply deadlines to keep you motivated. The deadlines should be challenging but realistic. You don't want to give yourself too little time to check something off, but you also don't want to give yourself too much time where it never happens. If I say I want to take sewing classes and know that it takes one year to get to the advanced classes, I'm not going to put down five months and stress myself out. Having a GPS gives you the push you need to work toward your goals on a regular basis and not just talk about them.

The LORD answered me, "Write the vision, and make it plain on tablets, that he who runs may read it." (Habakkuk 2:2)

CREATE A VISION BOARD

You have now done your research and created a plan. You are seeing things happen for you. Let's say I completed my sewing classes and have five new designs created. I've even had a focus group with family and friends on which scarves they like the best and how much they would pay for them. I'm excited because I'm making progress, but I can't stop there. Creating a visual representation of your dreams is a great way to keep you motivated and excited. This can be done by making a vision board.

A vision board is full of encouraging, inspiring, and motivating pictures and words cut out of magazines or printed from the internet and pasted on any size poster board or on a sheet of construction paper. You can decorate it with ribbon, glitter, fabric, and even put it in a frame. It is a fun activity to do in a group setting with friends or family. You can have food, beverages, and play good music, and then each person can present their boards to each other. Once it is complete, you can hang it in your room, locker, or on your desk at work. Each day I pray over my vision board and work toward reaching the goals I've set for myself. Seeing them every day keeps them at the forefront of your mind so you can manifest the destiny you see in front of you. If you don't at first see yourself getting there, you can't go. You can update your vision board as you check things off or even have multiple vision boards for different areas of your life.

BE CONSISTENT

Many people get to a certain point and quit for several reasons, but I think the top two are because the excitement wears off or they get distracted or discouraged. Sometimes even when you are certain God wants you to work toward a dream, you will get to a point where it isn't fun and is uncomfortable. The sign of a committed person is that they will push past the desire to quit. Sometimes you can take a break, do something that relaxes you, and face the discomfort head on. Being consistent means doing the right things over and over. It means you don't quit until you are finished the task. Distractions and discouragement will always come your way, but it will be up to you to recognize them for what they are and not be pulled in.

For instance, for the scarf business, say that I see another scarf company using a similar design that I planned on bringing out. Instead of giving in to the urge to scrap the entire collection, I would decide to add a unique spin to what the competition did so that my designs can stand out. People who turn their dreams into a reality learn very quickly how to turn a negative into a positive and don't allow anything to stop them on their journey to success.

If you want and love something, you continue to work at it until you turn what is in your mind to what is in your life. If what you say you want doesn't line up with what you are seeing, that means you aren't doing enough. Do something every day to chip away at your list. Refer to your GPS often to remind you of the steps you are taking. Check them off one by one and keep working. You got this.

> **Being confident of this, that he who began a good work in you will carry it on to completion until the day of Christ Jesus. (Philippians 1:6)**

TELL SOMEONE

I know you may not feel comfortable telling people about your goals and dreams. Many small-minded people we call Dream Killers will try to make you feel crazy, depending on how big your dream is. You'll be able to identify them if they ask negative questions and keep telling you how hard it is. Once you see this happening, don't even try explaining anything to them. They'll have to watch from the sidelines as you cross the finish line. Everyone can't go where God is taking you. Just like a train or a bus drops people off along the way, you'll have to do the same thing on the road to your destiny.

Other people will try to steal your goal or dream for themselves because they don't know what they are supposed to do with their own lives. Let's not worry about those people because what God has for you is for you. No matter how hard they try, as long as you stay focused and dedicated to your own plan, they can't stop you from reaching your goals nor can they make what is uniquely meant for you happen for themselves.

Find someone you can trust to share your dream with. This can be your best friend (a real one who cares about you and wants to see you win), a parent, your brother or sister, or even a teacher who has a genuine interest in your growth and development. Tell them what you want to do and when you want to do it. They can be there for you and encourage and motivate you, or they may know someone who has done something similar and can give you some great advice.

A coach or mentor is another way to keep you consistent. This is someone who knows what it is like to work hard toward and accomplish a goal. They have to be focused, resourceful, genuine, honest, encouraging, a good listener, and someone who has their head on straight. You want someone who has already overcome some of the obstacles in their way and can tell you how to avoid or work through those obstacles and get through the hard times.

> **So let's keep focused on that goal, those of us who want everything God has for us. If any of you have something else in mind, something less than total commitment, God will clear your blurred vision— you'll see it yet! Now that we're on the right track, let's stay on it. (Philippians 3:15-16)**

STAY FOCUSED

A lack of focus is the biggest issue that keeps people from reaching their goals and making their dreams come true. Distractions come from every direction in various forms. Sometimes the distractions are just for a few hours like a phone call from a friend about her new boyfriend or a television show that caught your attention. They may seem like small distractions until you add up one 30-minute call and one-hour-long show each day. That totals 10.5 hours (a full workday) that could have been spent reaching your goal.

Other distractions can come in the form of things you can't control—a breakup that can leave you feeling like the world will end, your parents' divorce, which causes all sorts of emotion and maybe even drama, a move that makes you feel intimidated as the new girl in school. All of those examples can take you off course and make you forget you even had a goal to begin with. Believe me, I've been there! So many times when I was starting a new business or planning a big event, something would happen in my personal life that would make me want to sleep through the day to escape the emotional rollercoaster. It helps when I give myself a deadline and keep reminding myself that I will see the finish line soon. I know that no matter what, I have to get it done, and skipping a day of work, study, planning, or action will pile on more for me to do the next day or the day after that.

You must have a focus so sharp that it doesn't give you room to dwell on distractions. Most times those things come just when you are gliding on the right path to success. Just when it seems like you have found your rhythm and get in a groove, here comes something to make you miss a beat. If you stay focused and keep your eye on the prize, knowing that better days are on the other side of the goal, you can drown out the noise to your left and right and only pay attention to the path you are on.

I know you want to have fun, hang out with your friends, and talk and laugh on the phone about nothing, but you can set a schedule every day to make sure you are spending more time on your goals than wasting it doing things that won't benefit your future.

CELEBRATE EACH MILESTONE

It is important to make sure that when you are headed to Dreamville (that is what we are calling it now), you celebrate each small milestone. A milestone is when you've reached a goal or something big happens to move you to a new level in your journey.

For example, say I wanted to start selling the scarves and my goal was to make $1,500 each week by the end of the year. I ordered them wholesale, created a website, and launched the business. Within a few months, I started making 20 sales a week that made me $500 each week. That milestone should be celebrated. To get to $1,500, you had to have at least $500 in sales at some point, so it is a stepping-stone. Instead of saying, "Dang, it has been months and I still am not at $1,000 . . . I have a long way to go," celebrate the fact that you have made more than you did when you started. Then celebrate every small goal you meet.

The race is not won to the swift but to the one who endureth till the end. (Ecclesiastes 9:11)

Imagine a runner in a race. She is tired, hot, thirsty, and there is a cramp in her leg throbbing so bad she wants to cry. Imagine her family and friends on the other side of the finish line waiting to cheer her through that line. She has about five minutes of running left when someone yells at her, *"You're a loser; you won't make it! You look like you're in pain! You might as well quit!"* Instead of looking straight at the finish line, she wants to fight the person and gets totally sidetracked and loses the race! All that practice and preparation went down the drain the minute she took her focus off the goal and put it on something that had nothing to do with what she wanted. Don't be that girl! Be the girl who stays focused and wins the race God has given her to run no matter how it looks on the way to the finish line.

NEVER QUIT

So you've learned how to manage distractions on the way to making your dreams come true, but the dream will surely die if you quit. Yes, you can avoid wasting time, but when it feels like what you are trying to accomplish is impossible, it is very important that you decide to never quit. To quit means to abandon. Have you ever been riding through a neighborhood that has boarded up homes or buildings? The grass isn't cut, the windows are either busted out or covered with plastic or wood, trash is in the yard, and bricks or siding is missing. I remember going to a neighborhood that had beautiful homes and one home looked just like that. I introduced myself to a neighbor and asked if she knew what happened to that particular house. She said the owner suddenly abandoned the project and moved to another city with family after some financial issues. The house looked sad, empty, and forgotten. Don't allow your dreams to be forgotten and abandoned just because things happen in your life on your way to success. If you stay focused and never quit, you can make your dreams come true.

You need a lot of faith and prayer to reach your goals, whether big or small. With so many things that come at you on a daily basis, you need to keep God as the foundation of all of your dreams and goals. Prayer will also keep you in communication with God. He is your compass through all of this, and since prayer is not just talking to God and includes listening, He will speak to you about the details that make your dream specific to you. Keep a pen and pad with you during prayer. Anyone can have a general dream, but a custom-made dream just for you comes from God. Say this prayer with your dreams in mind to stay motivated and encouraged even through the rough times.

PRAYER

Father, in the name of Jesus, thank you so much for putting a dream in my heart and giving me the desire and motivation to make it happen with you by my side. I ask that you protect my dream from negative people and continue to guide me even when I feel like I can't go on. I rebuke doubt, fear, discouragement, and distractions in Jesus' name! I thank you for giving me creativity, energy, enthusiasm, strength, grace, a consistent heart, and crazy faith to get this done! Amen.

EMOTIONS

A hot-tempered man stirs up strife, but he who is slow to anger quiets contention. (Proverbs 15:18)

So if you can't always act on what you are feeling and have to keep your emotions under control, why do you have them in the first place? God gave you emotions to experience life to the fullest and connect to others. Emotions also let you know how you feel about a situation or something that is happening to you. For example, if something negative happens in your life like being mistreated or disrespected, your emotions will tell you, *"This doesn't feel right. I don't like it."* Or if something positive happens to you like you just walked in on your own surprise party, your emotions tell you, *"OMG, this is so amazing. I feel so loved and happy."*

While this is great, it is important to keep your emotions in check so you can respond to them in a healthy way and make good decisions. If you allow your emotions to rule you instead of the other way around, you will cause yourself a lot of trouble and may come off as unstable, with no discipline or self-control. People who lack self-control and discipline are looked at as dangerous and untrustworthy. Have you ever met someone who seems to be all over the place? Have you ever felt like you are on an emotional rollercoaster—up one day, down the next? You're shouting "positive vibes only" one week, and as soon as something happens, you're back feeling mad, confused, or depressed. God wants so much better for you, and you can get ahold of your emotions and be stable, steady, and set free from falling apart at every twist and turn life takes you through.

WHAT ARE YOU FEELING?

The first step in rising above your emotions is figuring out what you're feeling in the first place. If your friend said something mean about your new hairstyle, are you sad because she didn't consider your feelings or are you angry because she made you feel insecure? It is important to realize what emotion is going through your body so you can react in the right way. If you are sad, then you can express that by telling the person they hurt you. If you are angry, you have to then figure out the source of the anger. Take a second to respond so you can process the feeling before clapping back or responding negatively.

Back before I knew Jesus for real, I would fly off the handle no matter what emotion I felt. If my feelings were hurt, I'd yell and cut them off immediately. If I was sad, I would cry and feel sorry for myself and rehearse what happened over and over in my mind. If I was angry, I would cuss, fuss, and fight. If I was frustrated, I would be easily irritated and let anything ruin my day. I didn't know how to process my emotions and was a hot mess most of the time. What I was feeling may have been valid, but I didn't know how to properly process those feelings, so I was always on edge and my mood changed like the weather. When my emotions made me uncomfortable, I had to get it out. I thought if I didn't let it be known what I was feeling, I was letting people get away with something. You may be going through something similar, but it is possible to mature into an emotionally responsible, stable young woman who knows how to process her emotions in a healthy way.

SAY IT; DON'T SPRAY IT

Have you ever seen someone sneeze and not cover their mouth? You can literally see the germs spraying everywhere and landing on whatever is nearby. Ugh. Imagine now that when you go off or react to a negative emotion, it is like sneezing without covering your mouth. Your attitude affects everyone and has the power to spread and infect. The second step in dealing with emotions is to learn to communicate your emotions in a way that doesn't make everyone sick. Take these steps to communicate without attacking anyone or walking around with an attitude.

- Think five times before you speak. Literally say what you are thinking five times to yourself and change your words if necessary before speaking them.
- Watch your tone. Don't raise your voice or start yelling. Take a deep breath and remain calm. No one will receive your words just because they are loud.
- Practice your words with a friend or family member. Ask for their feedback.
- Picture yourself speaking to someone you would never want to disrespect.

👑 If the person you are speaking with is being disrespectful, immediately end the conversation in a cool and calm manner. Wish them the best and walk away until you both cool down. If that never happens, give the issue to God and let it go. Allowing yourself to be caught up in a toxic cycle does a lot of damage to your emotions.

Everyone around you will respect you more when you use words in a kind tone that lets them know how you feel without hurting or attacking them and causing more drama. Yes, you're upset. Yes, you feel a certain type of way, but you can say things without spraying negativity on everyone. It is okay to have emotions, and you have a right to feel how you feel when you experience things, good and bad. However, the last thing you want is to be known as a hothead or someone who is out of control. The next time you are feeling something negative, take a deep breath, close your eyes if you have to or even walk away for a second, identify the emotion, let yourself feel it, and then come up with the right words to communicate it.

My grandmother always said, "You can catch more flies with honey than you can with vinegar." Now I have no idea why anyone would want to catch flies, but I do understand that honey tastes much sweeter than vinegar. Sweet words will give you a sweet response, but sour words will get you a sour response. When someone makes you angry or disrespects you, the last thing you want to do is treat them sweetly, but the Bible says in 1 Peter 3:9, *"Do not repay evil with evil or insult with insult. On the contrary, repay evil with blessing, because to this you were called so that you may inherit a blessing."* There is a reward for not seeking revenge, whether it is with your words or hands.

When someone is mistreating you, you cannot respond the way everyone else does. You have to respond the way God wants. Pastor Mike Freeman, my former pastor, says, "Your response is your responsibility." God will deal with the person who did you wrong, but if you stoop to their level, God will have to deal with you too for being in the wrong and disobeying His Word. Be found doing the right thing by following the four steps to rise above your emotions. As a reminder, I've listed the first three here:

1. Identify the correct emotion
2. Process the emotion
3. Properly communicate the emotion

Lay aside bitter words, temper tantrums, revenge, profanity, and insults. But instead be kind and affectionate toward one another. Has God graciously forgiven you? Then graciously forgive one another in the depths of Christ's love. (Ephesians 4:31-32)

RELEASE AND FORGIVE

The last step is releasing the emotion through prayer and forgiveness. This is the most important step. God is a forgiving God, and even if you mess up the first three steps, this last step is key because it makes sure you are not walking around with bottled up emotions you have never released to God. Unforgiveness can make you physically and spiritually sick and can cause you to block your blessings. So many people are walking around angry, frustrated, or sad from things that happened to them 5, 20, and even 50 years ago. They lose friends and family due to their bad attitudes, constantly play the victim at their jobs and churches, and feel sorry for themselves because they never learned how to release the bad emotions and totally forgive the person who made them feel that way. Sometimes they even walk around mad at God for allowing whatever happened to them.

Now, traumatic things certainly happen to people in their childhood or even in adulthood that cause them to grow bitterness in their heart. An experience like the death of a loved one, constant abuse or bullying, or heartbreak or betrayal can cause people to build up resentment and walk around angry. Sometimes they even end up dying with regret and disappointment, never fully living the life they could have lived. Unforgiveness and unresolved emotions can affect every area of your life, but if you follow the steps, you can be free.

When you find yourself struggling to let something go, it means you haven't released the emotion in your soul. Your soul is your mind, will, and emotions. You can tell the trauma hasn't been released if you do any, some, or all of the following things:

- ♕ Having dreams and rehearsing what happened over and over
- ♕ Can't stop talking about the issue and telling everyone who will listen, even strangers, what happened to you
- ♕ Think of the person and instantly get angry all over again, like it just happened five minutes ago
- ♕ Thinking of how to get revenge or being happy to hear that the person isn't doing well

~~~~~~

I will give you the keys of the kingdom of heaven; whatever you bind on earth will be bound in heaven, and whatever you loose on earth will be loosed in heaven. (Matthew 16:19)

~~~~~~

Once you admit to yourself that it is not over in your soul, you have to do some binding and loosing. You can release the negative emotions and bring in the positive qualities whenever you want, and God gave you the authority to do that. These are the words to say to release bad emotions:

I choose as an act of my will to loose _____ out of my soul. I loose the trauma that _____ caused. I choose as an act of my will to bind the joy of the Lord, the peace of God, purity, healing, holiness, wholeness, and love in Jesus' name to my soul! I forgive _____ in the name of Jesus and release them from what they did to me in Jesus' name!

Once you do this, you can be free to live a life that is emotionally balanced and full of the right emotions in your heart while processing the wrong things out of your heart in a healthy and righteous manner.

PRAYER

Father, in the name of Jesus, thank you for your unending love for me. Thank you for forgiving me whenever I mess up. Because of the brand-new mercies you give me every day, you require me to forgive others fully in my heart. It's hard when they make me feel bad, sad, or angry, but I know I can do all things through you. Give me the strength to release the negative emotions, work through the pain, and forgive those who hurt me or cause me pain. Amen.

FRIENDSHIP

Reliable friends who do what they say are like cool drinks in sweltering heat—refreshing!
(Proverbs 25:13)

My definition of a friend is someone you share a close bond with and can trust, someone who sharpens you but gives you room to be yourself, is there when you need them, and doesn't compete with you. It is important to know what makes a good friend so you can choose them wisely. Sometimes you may want to be someone's friend so badly that you ignore the things that don't make them a good friend. A friendship should make both people feel comfortable. If you feel like your friend is the only one benefitting from the friendship and you are left hanging, then maybe the situation isn't what you thought. Friends can motivate you, stand up for you, give you advice and support, and even boost your mood. This doesn't mean friendships are always perfect, but when two people care about each other, issues can be fixed with communication and consideration. Let's go over the qualities you should look for in a friend so you won't mistake a person who wants a favor for a person who wants a friend.

A friend loves at all times. (Proverbs 17:17)

TOP FIVE FRIENDSHIP QUALITIES

I've chosen five qualities that you should have to be a good friend and that you should look for in a friend. These qualities deal with a person's core. You know when you bite into an apple and see brown, rotten, and mushy spots? Most of the time it started with the core, and it can't be eaten. I've learned that if the core of a person is rotten, their relationships will be rotten. Eating from the plate of a rotten person will poison you. If a person is spiritually rotten and has no morals, you'll be spiritually poisoned. If someone is emotionally rotten and plays mind games and tries to trick you, there is a good chance you will be emotionally poisoned. That doesn't mean they can't change or improve, and you can pray for them, but I wouldn't put them at the top of my friendship pile. The following qualities will help you distinguish the people who want to add to your life from the people who want to subtract.

Honest: Trustworthy, Genuine, Sincere, Direct

Honesty is one of the most important qualities of a friend, even if hearing or telling the truth is uncomfortable. Your friends should nicely tell the truth instead of lying. For example, if you get a new dress and it doesn't fit right, your friend should be sensitive to your feelings but direct with the truth. Instead of saying, "You look ugly in that dress!" they should say, "I think a dress with peplum would flatter your figure better." If you find out your friend is lying to others, they probably will lie to you too. True friends won't try to steal your boyfriend, your job, or your personality. They will let you know when they're concerned about your bad habit or behavior and do their best to stick up for you when you're in trouble.

If you want to be a good friend, make sure you not only tell the truth to your friends but let your actions be true. If you don't want to do something, be honest. If you have other plans when your friends ask to do something, tell them right then; don't pretend you will make it. If you give your word or make a promise, keep it. Trust is the glue that holds any friendship together, and every time you do the opposite of what you say you will do, the glue gets weaker and the friendship can fall apart.

You also have to be willing to hear the truth. If God blesses you with an honest friend who has your best interest at heart, but you get mad each time they tell you the truth, that is not being a good friend.

Consistent: Dependable, Steady, Reliable, True

Consistency is key in friendships. It means repeating positive behavior, which builds trust and momentum. You can't rely on someone who keeps you guessing about whether they will be there for you. Real friends don't switch up on you. One day they like you; the next day they are whispering behind your back or making you feel confused about where you stand with them. Friends will start to resent you if you constantly let them down.

I had to cut off my best friend a few years ago because she was so unreliable. After a while, she didn't even try to keep her word. We used to do everything together like going to dinner, talking all day every day, and celebrating birthdays together. As we got older, I noticed some things that didn't feel like friendship to me. If we made plans, she would show up late or not at all. One time she agreed to go to an event with me, but she needed a ride. I drove an hour in traffic to get her, and when I got to the traffic light right before her house, I called to tell her to come outside. She said, "Girl, I'm tired. I decided not to go." I was so mad and stopped asking her to go places with me unless she could drive.

The second strike was when we went to a church event and on the way back, my car started acting up. I called my mechanic, and he said it would take an hour to get to me, so I pulled over on the side of the road. Within seconds, she was on the phone with someone asking them to come get her instead of waiting with me. It started getting dark and cold outside, and since my car wouldn't start, the heat wasn't working. I had to call another friend to come sit with me because the mechanic took a little longer. I finally made it home that night, and she didn't even call and check to see if I made it home. I didn't speak to her for months! We finally started speaking again, and that was the worst decision I could have made. For another year, I opened myself up to more disappointment, regret, and broken promises. This friend took advantage of me one last time, and I ended the friendship once and for all. I haven't seen or talked to her since, and I'm not missing out at all.

If you've tried to talk to your friend about their bad behavior or lack of effort in your friendship and they don't do anything to change or make an excuse saying, "That's just how I am!" then that is not the friend for you. Wish them the best and leave them alone. You will not regret it. Stop giving people second chances to mistreat you. The more you do this, the less respect they will have for you and the more disappointed you will be when they do something else to show you that your feelings don't matter. No matter how good our conversations were, how long we were friends, or how much fun we had when we were together, she showed me over and over that she was not consistent or considerate. I should have walked away from that flimsy friendship long before I did.

Supportive: Encouraging, Caring, Understanding, Helpful, Protective, Kind

Being supportive in bad times is important, but being supportive of others in their good times is just as important. For example, if your friend has an important audition and you can help her practice, that is being supportive. If your friend is nervous about a job interview or is working on a big project, sending a text to encourage her or calling and praying with her is great too. When she gets that job, bake her a cake or post it on Facebook! If you have trouble celebrating your friend's good days and get jealous, you will have a hard time keeping friends. On the other hand, if your friend wants your life and can't ever celebrate your accomplishments, that won't be a good friend. Supportive friends make you stronger, let you cry on their shoulder, and pray for you regularly. If you notice you are being supportive and your friend rarely supports you, decide if that is something you can deal with. Friendships should never be one-sided.

Loyal: Faithful, Devoted, Real, and Solid

Loyalty keeps bonds strong and is at the top of the list of qualities you should have and want in a friend. A loyal friend will stick with you even if they meet a new friend. A loyal friend will be by your side if you make a mistake. A loyal friend won't tell your business or talk about you behind your back. Be loyal and get loyalty back. Be someone who folds as easily as a piece of paper and people will fold on you. A loyal friend won't judge you and make you feel bad when you are struggling with something. They will be there for you through thick and thin.

Respectful: Considerate, Thoughtful, Attentive, and Polite

Being respectful means being sensitive to your friend's feelings and allowing them to express themselves. If your friend is going through something and wants to chill by herself, respect her need for space and don't demand what you want. Respectful friends don't get mad when their friends have other friends. Friends are people, not possessions. You can't own a person, so you can't make them do what you want them to do nor can you use or abuse them. If your friend disrespects your boundaries and always finds a way to make you feel less than, examine the friendship. You deserve better.

> **Don't be naive. There are difficult times ahead. As the end approaches, people will be self-absorbed, money-hungry, self-promoting, stuck-up, profane, contemptuous of parents, crude, coarse, dog-eat-dog, unbending, slanderers, impulsively wild, savage, cynical, treacherous, ruthless, bloated windbags, addicted to lust, and allergic to God. They'll make a show of religion, but behind the scenes they're animals. Stay clear of these people. (2 Timothy 3:1-5)**

BAD FRIENDS

Be careful when choosing friends. Some people weren't raised right, and their goal is to use or get as much out of people as possible.

Others get sick, twisted joy by causing others pain. They have been hurt and need healing and deliverance. If you've already been treated badly and think it is better to stay to yourself, it is not. It is never better to be alone because of one person. You can't give them that type of power over your life and choices. Pray for them, forgive them, and leave them in the past. Don't even look back. God will replace them with real friends.

> **A man that hath friends must shew himself friendly. (Proverbs 18:24)**

HOW TO MAKE FRIENDS

The first step in making new friends is not just about introducing yourself. It is knowing who you are first. This way you will know the type of people you will get along with. Make a list of the things you like to do with friends and what kind of friend you are and then another list of the type of friend you want. Memorize that list so that when you meet someone, you can tell if you have things in common with them.

Meeting people can be hard, especially if you're shy, but you may click with some of your friends' friends. If someone at school invites you to an event and you don't think you'll know anyone, go anyway. If you see someone by themselves, introduce yourself, smile, and compliment them. Everyone loves receiving compliments, and they help break the ice.

When you meet someone new, start a conversation and ask open-ended questions. Open-ended questions give you more than one-word answers like yes or no. Instead of asking "Do you like to swim?" ask

"What are some of your favorite things to do?" Instead of asking "Do you have any brothers or sisters?" say "Tell me about your family." These types of questions help you get to know someone better and show that you actually care about finding out the things that matter.

Another way to make new friends is to join a class or club. If you like music or are an athlete, this is a sure-fire way of getting to know people who share a common interest. It is important to be approachable. If you have a mean or sour look on your face that says, "Don't even try it," you may be labeled as unfriendly before anyone has a chance to talk to you. You don't have to change who you are to make friends, but you definitely shouldn't look like you are ready to fight anybody who tries to speak.

When making friends, remember to set boundaries—lines that you should never allow anyone to cross if they call you their friend. Some examples of boundaries are:

- Friends don't hit each other, whether playing or not.
- Friends don't tell each other's business.
- Friends don't call each other degrading names.
- Friends don't let each other down.
- Friends don't use or take advantage of each other.

What are some of your boundaries—the things you refuse to allow? If it doesn't feel right, chances are it isn't right. If a friend is always talking about their other friends, they are probably talking about you too. Some people aren't looking for real friends but for someone to do their hair for free, borrow clothes from, and use them for anything they can get their hands on. They aren't looking for love. They are looking for a favor. Stay away from these kinds of people. They are not to be trusted.

COMMUNICATION IN FRIENDSHIP

Communication is giving and receiving information. It is how we understand each other. It can be verbal with words like "You are nice," "I like your clothes," or "You are so funny!" It can also be nonverbal with facial expressions like a smile or a frown. Another form of nonverbal communication is body language like crossing our arms or turning our back. All of these things send a message. No one should have to guess what you are feeling. It is important to get comfortable saying what is on your mind in a calm and respectful way. You should be able to talk to your friend about what bothers you.

Think twice about how you approach someone. It may make things worse. I like to say "keep it cute." You should first talk, then listen to understand, think about what was said, and then respond. If you find it hard to say what you mean, sometimes writing a letter will work. Never discuss something important over text. Face-to-face conversation is best, and the telephone is second best. You can't keep up a healthy friendship without proper communication. It doesn't mean you have to talk 10x a day every day, but you should be consistent in order to stay close.

POSITIVE COMMUNICATION

To have good and long-lasting friendships, you should attempt to keep communication positive. If your friend hurts your feelings, be direct and honest. Don't go telling everybody else before talking to your friend. Matthew 18:15 says, ***"If your (sister) sins against you, go and tell (her what she's done), between you and (her) alone. If she listens to you, you have gained your (sister)."*** I changed the words to apply to a friend. If your friend doesn't listen or dismisses your feelings, it may be time to reevaluate the friendship. You deserve to be heard and under-stood at all times.

Other forms of positive communication include:

- ♛ **Prayer** – You should pray with and for your friends. This will draw you closer to each other and form a bond that nobody can break.

- ♛ **Encouragement** – This will make her feel better in hard times.

- ♛ **Compliments** – This will build your friend's confidence.

- ♛ **Jokes** – The Bible says that laughter is like medicine (Proverbs 17:22).

- ♛ Can you come up with more positive ways to communicate with your friend?

NEGATIVE COMMUNICATION

You should stay away from negative communication, including mean criticism and insults. Proverbs 15:4 says, ***"Kind words heal and help; cutting words wound and maim."*** To maim means to injure. Would you want to injure your good friend? Gossiping is another thing you should stay far away from. I know sipping and spilling tea is the cool and fun thing to do. Millions of people follow blogs and message boards that tell everybody's business. People who gossip cannot be trusted. If someone comes to you with gossip, tell them you don't have time to talk about someone else; you have your own life to deal with. Picture gossip as a can of trash. Now picture someone dumping that trash all over you. Now you are filthy and stinky. That is what gossip does. Ephesians 4:29 says, ***"Watch the way you talk. Let nothing foul or dirty come out of your mouth. Say only what helps, each word a gift."*** This not only includes gossip but also cursing and yelling. Would you give or want to receive a dirty, rotten gift? I don't think so. If each word is a gift, you should only be speaking kind, thoughtful, and loving words.

Friendship is a beautiful thing, but it takes effort and energy to keep it going. As you grow and mature, you'll see that some friends are not meant to last a lifetime. Some only last for a season, like while you are in the same class or school. Others last during a time you needed them most, but there are friends who will last forever. When you find a great friend who has the qualities discussed and you feel like your best self with that person, hold on to that friend and be good to them. Don't take them for granted. Don't mistreat them. Show them your appreciation. If they like earrings, buy them some and write a card. If they like a certain type of ice cream, have it at your house in case they hang out there a lot. Write a card or a nice text to thank them for always being there for you. If they want you to take their picture when they are feeling extra cute, take it without complaining and rolling your eyes. Let your friends know how much they mean to you and never let small things come between you.

PRAYER

Father, in the name of Jesus, thank you for calling me your friend and always being here for me. I want to learn how to be as good of a friend as you. Thank you for giving me the wisdom to pick good friends and not ignore red flags. Help me be a good friend by developing in me the qualities I need in my friendships like kindness, loyalty, and honesty. When someone I trust shows me they aren't my friend, help me forgive them and move on. Send only true friends my way and help me learn from the people who don't show themselves friendly. I love and praise you for the gift of friendship. Amen.

GRATITUDE

Oh, give thanks to the Lord, for he is good, for his steadfast love endures forever! (Psalms 107:1)

People think being grateful just means saying thank you when someone does something for you, but it means so much more than that. Gratitude rhymes with attitude, and it means living a thankful and appreciative life. When you look at life with gratitude, you find the blessing in everything. There are several ways to live a life of gratitude and watch it change your perspective from the inside out. When you are grateful for the things, people, and opportunities God has blessed you with, you can make the most of every day and view things in a positive light even when things aren't sunny and bright. Everyone goes through hard times. They are a part of life, but it is all in how you look at them.

GRATITUDE GLASSES

I like to call it putting on your Gratitude Glasses when you look at life with appreciation and thankfulness no matter what is going on in your life. I recently visited the eye doctor. I've been working on the computer since I was a teenager and noticed my vision was blurred when trying to read something up close. The doctor said I still have 20/20 vision, which is supposed to be perfect. However, I needed reading glasses because the strain of the computer was causing my eyes to get tired and burn out by the end of the day. He also said it is important to wear glasses with UV protection when you are on the computer or phone a lot. So I ordered some cute glasses and waited for them to come from the lab.

A couple of weeks later, as soon as I put the glasses on, my vision got clearer, more magnified, and that strain I felt went away. The same thing happens when you put on Gratitude Glasses. This doesn't mean your problems don't exist or magically disappear. It means you choose to focus on what is positive in your life and stop giving what is negative any power. Gratitude makes everything brighter and clearer and brings your blessings closer to your memory. Instead of complaining about what you don't have, when you wear your Gratitude Glasses, you see what you do have.

If you focus on the positive, that is what you will attract. If you focus on the negative, that is the only thing you will see. What you focus on gets bigger. Gratitude helps you focus on the good and minimize the bad. You know that God is bigger than any problem you have, so you can focus on your blessings and His goodness, and the negative won't have as much power.

COUNT YOUR BLESSINGS

Until the day she passed in 2007, my grandmother, Betty F. Massey, was my best friend. I could call her about anything. As a teenager, if my parents were being too hard on me, I called her to talk to them for me. When I had a bad day at school, she prayed with me. When I didn't feel like I was good enough, she encouraged me. She always knew just what to say or do.

Things were a bit different when I called her to complain about minor things though. "Granny, today was awful . . . I had to change for Phys Ed, and my cycle started, but the teacher still didn't let me sit out. I can't stand P.E. class." As I went on and on complaining, the first thing she would say after hearing me out was, "Did you count your blessings today?" The first time she asked me this, I was like, "No, of course not . . . I never even thought to do that." After a few times, I had to admit that I forgot to do this simple but powerful exercise. Then one day I finally agreed to do it.

Granny told me to take a piece of paper and write down everything I could think of to be thankful for that day. The rule was that I couldn't write down material things. This made it even harder because that is usually the first thing we think to write down. Because we have a lot of things, we think we are blessed, but what about the people who don't have as much as you? Does it mean they aren't blessed? No, it doesn't!

So here I was calling my grandmother, wanting her to agree that my life was awful because of what I felt was an emergency. But I got off the phone with what felt like a homework assignment. And of course, she told me to call her when I was done so I could read it to her. I would start the list big mad because I didn't want to do it in the first place. My list started off real dry like "food, sisters, brother, mom and dad, grandmother and grandfather, aunt and uncles" just to fill up the list. I then started getting into it and writing things like "my A in Creative Writing class," "clean water to drink," "I can walk on my own," "I'm healthy," and "my grade came up in math." By the time I called my grandmother back to read her my list, I had written about 30 things and forgot why I was even upset in the first place. The next morning, I woke up thanking God for the things I wrote down the night before, and my day went by smoothly even though I was still on my cycle and I still had PE class. I couldn't believe something like this worked so fast, and to this day, I still do it.

These days, people like to call my Granny's exercise a gratitude journal. Studies show that the benefit is an increase of positive vibes because it helps you see the good side of things and takes your mind off the negative things that happen. A gratitude journal improves self-esteem by reminding you of your personal achievements. When you feel like you aren't at your best, you can go back to your gratitude journal and read some of your accomplishments like "I won the track meet today" or "I got so many compliments on the new outfit I put together."

Studies also show that filling out your gratitude journal at night before bed takes your mind off your worries and clears it for a good night's rest. It also reduces stress and makes you feel more optimistic. You can literally change your life when you change your mind about how you look at things. I encourage you to start a gratitude journal today and see the benefits it brings.

Do all things without grumbling or questioning. (Philippians 2:14)

THE NO-COMPLAINT CHALLENGE

Complaining is an enemy to gratitude and puts you in the wrong mindset. You can't be productive while complaining. You can't be a witness to God's goodness while complaining, and you definitely can't be grateful if you are complaining. Have you ever been around someone who always complains? Do you feel drained around them? Have you ever found yourself in a negative mood one day and all you can do is complain? Complaining is letting it be known out loud how disappointed or annoyed you are about something. Retrain your brain to stop complaining and start celebrating even the smallest of blessings.

Yes, life gets messy sometimes. Depending on what age you are, you haven't even seen how messy it can get. Hopefully, this book helps you avoid the things I went through as I got older, but even for the nicest, most focused young lady, it isn't always sunshine and butterflies. I know your parents don't always see your point of view, and if you have siblings, I understand how much of a pain they can be sometimes. I know your teachers get on your nerves and friends even disappoint you at times. School gets rough, bad days exist, and it is easy to get into a rut and feel sorry for yourself and vent to anyone listening how awful your life seems. But today is a new day! You will complain less and celebrate more!

Complaining is pointless because it doesn't change the situation. What you focus on will expand, so if you focus on the things that cause grief, sadness, or frustration, that is what will become bigger. If you focus on a solution and how you can overcome the difficulty, what is possible and positive will expand.

Each day, I want you to start with gratitude, whether you're praying and thanking God in the morning for opening your eyes and allowing you to see another day or ending your night by writing in your gratitude journal. Challenge yourself and your friends not to complain. Each time you complain, you have to find something else to celebrate. If you got a B- on a paper you know you put your all into, celebrate the fact that you are even in your right mind to write a paper. Some girls your age are in the hospital right now, diagnosed with cancer and wishing they could go to school. So look at the bright side of things and stop complaining.

When you complain less and celebrate more, you can work through the issues you face with a positive mindset. Tough times don't last, so there is no sense in treating each situation like it's permanent and final and allowing it to take you off your square.

> **Give thanks to the Lord, for He is good. His love endures forever. (Psalms 136:1)**

The never-changing truth that God is good and that He will love us forever is enough reason to celebrate. He gives us life, health, strength, protection, love, and so many blessings. He is your Heavenly Father, and a good father won't let his child suffer for too long. He is right there, and as long as you keep the faith and look at things through the lenses of your Gratitude Glasses, you will start to notice that even on a bumpy road, you can find something to be thankful for.

GIVE BACK

Giving back is very important to me. I believe it not only keeps you humble but makes you feel even more appreciative of what you have. If you truly want to develop an attitude of gratitude, start to volunteer on a monthly basis. You can go to a local soup kitchen to feed the homeless, make Thanksgiving and Christmas boxes for the needy, organize a coat drive, read to children at a hospital, or even spend time at a senior citizen home. I love talking to the elderly. They have so many stories and words of wisdom to pour into you. When you get new clothes, you can bag up the old ones that everybody has already seen on social media or at a big event. Instead of randomly giving a big bag of clothes away, bag them up and ask friends, family, neighbors, classmates, and co-workers if they know of anyone who wears your size and would appreciate some gently used items.

There are so many ways to give back. It not only makes you feel good inside, but it definitely helps put your problems in perspective, helps you be more others-minded, and shows that you have a lot to be grateful for.

PRAYER

Father, in the name of Jesus, thank you so much for giving me another opportunity to show my appreciation and gratitude for being in the land of the living. So many people didn't wake up this morning, but you saw fit for me to not only wake up but be in my right mind, have all the activity of my limbs, and be able to strive to fulfill the purpose you created me to fulfill. Father, I am so sorry and repent for all the times I seemed ungrateful and complained instead of looking at the many things you blessed me with. From this day forward, I will wear my Gratitude Glasses and remind myself of the amazing life I have by writing in my gratitude journal. I will complain less and celebrate more. Remind me when I am off track and give me a grateful heart so I can be a witness of your love and mercy everywhere I go. Amen!

HYGIENE

*P*aul urges us to present our bodies as a living sacrifice, holy and pleasing to God. What sort of body do you offer as you live for him? You cannot always avoid sickness but are you making the best use of your resources, both physically as well as spiritually? Are others put at risk by your poor hygiene? Is this a Christian attitude? (Philippians 2:4)

What do you think of when you see the word hygiene? Brushing your teeth? Taking a shower? Washing your face? That's part of it, but you must make sure you are doing these things like a Queen. A Queen takes her time on grooming and keeping up with hygiene. If you are rolling out of bed 10 minutes before you leave the house, you either have a glam squad waiting for you or your hygiene routine is lacking.

CROWNING GLORY (HAIR CARE)

Whether you are wearing weave, a wig, your natural curls, a silk press, braids, or crochets, it is very important to take care of your real hair underneath. Wash your hair with a sulfate-free shampoo that moisturizes and conditions your hair properly. Use wild growth for edge health and oil your scalp if it is dry. Your hair should stay conditioned and moisturized. Stay away from products with alcohol. It is important to do protein treatments that strengthen your hair and to get trims every 8-10 weeks. Walking around with raggedy ends and dandruff is not cute, and people will not be able to take you seriously if you look like you don't take care of yourself.

SAVE FACE

The first step to a glowing complexion is to figure out what type of skin you have and then use the products that best fit. Beauty products can have a lot of junk in them that isn't good for you, so please make sure to look for natural, paraben-free ingredients that will not poison your system or be too rough on your skin. I love to use The Ordinary products. They are affordable and effective.

Below is a list of skin types and how you can tell if you fall into that category.

- **Normal skin**: Balanced, not too dry, not too oily, no blemishes or acne, small pores
- **Dry Skin**: Scaly, flaky, tightness, and maybe even itchy
- **Oily Skin:** Large pores, shiny, blackheads, and whiteheads
- **Acne-Prone Skin:** Cystic bumps, enlarged pores, dark blemishes
- **Sensitive Skin:** Redness, burning, itching, allergy-prone
- **Combination Skin:** Oily T-zone with enlarged pores, normal to dry cheeks

Skin Tips

- Use at least SPF 15 that blocks UVB/UVA rays.

- 👑 Avoid extremely hot water on your face.
- 👑 Wash your face gently but completely by counting backward from 30 seconds and massaging it.
- 👑 Avoid using rough-textured washcloths to wash or dry your face.
- 👑 Sleep on a satin pillowcase.
- 👑 Drink plenty of water every day.
- 👑 Never ever sleep with makeup on your face.
- 👑 Don't pop your pimples.
- 👑 Make sure your hands are clean when you touch your face.
- 👑 Eat a healthy diet (see Nourishment Chapter).
- 👑 Exercise regularly.
- 👑 Use a face mask every day.
- 👑 Steam your skin by holding your face (not too close) over a bowl or a pot of hot water for 15 minutes.
- 👑 Get your beauty rest.
- 👑 Avoid drugs, cigarettes, and alcohol. It makes you ugly and bloated.
- 👑 Apply moisturizer. Use oil-free for oily or acne-prone skin.

MIND YOUR MOUTH

Flossing is just as important as brushing. To get all the gunk from food stuck between your teeth, you should floss every day after every meal. If you don't, it will create bacteria and smell so bad that it will scare even the strongest nose away. The next time you floss, smell it and you'll see what I mean. I know it sounds disgusting but imagine that odor multiplying after several missed days of flossing. You don't want to be the one to have people say about you, "That girl is coming with the stank breath."

Your toothbrush can't get to everything in there, so if you don't floss it out, it'll just sit there and can cause cavities and gum disease. You'll walk around with teeth missing. The first step to avoiding that is to floss. You can pick up a pack of floss picks (not the old-fashioned string because nobody uses that anymore) at Dollar Tree. Carry them with you in your purse and make sure to floss after each meal.

Invest in a water flosser to use once or twice a week. You can use water or peroxide to deep clean your mouth and get anything regular floss and brushing won't get. You'll be surprised what more will come out and your dentist will be proud of you. You should be seeing him or her every six months to get the deep cleaning your mouth deserves.

Brushing after every meal is a good rule, especially when you have braces. When that is not possible, make sure to floss, and you can carry some mouthwash in your purse to gargle in the bathroom at school or work. You definitely want to brush every morning and before bed. You need a good toothbrush with medium bristles and toothpaste that has a whitening agent. I use TheraBreath. It doesn't have alcohol, but it cleans thoroughly and has a matching mouthwash.

Tips for Brushing:

- Place your toothbrush at an angle that covers your teeth and gums.
- Move the brush gently in tooth-wide strokes.
- Brush the outer, inner, and chewing surfaces (all around including the back teeth).

👑 Don't forget to brush your tongue and the roof of your mouth. It freshens your breath while getting rid of bacteria. Buy a tongue scraper from Dollar Tree.

Mouthwash is the last step in the Mind Your Mouth routine. In my research, I found out that mouthwash is a temporary fix. If you don't brush or floss very well, mouthwash will cover up the odor for about 30 minutes, and then your mouth will snitch on you. Using one with fluoride is recommended by most dentists to prevent decay and freshen breath. However, many of those contain alcohol, and I don't like swishing alcohol around in my mouth for any amount of time. It causes dry mouth and oral cancer, and I'd like to avoid those things at all costs. Look for alcohol-free mouthwash or use peroxide.

THE ART OF BATHING (AND SHOWERING)

I know taking a shower is fast and convenient. You can rinse off everything and watch it go down the drain, but taking a bath is not only relaxing but a good soak of your lady parts is necessary after that time of the month. After your cycle, you should soak two days back to back for at least 30 minutes in a warm tub of water with one cup of Apple cider vinegar added. Never ever douche or spray anything up your vagina. You'll pay dearly with infections, dryness, or a pH imbalance. Once you soak, take a shower and use the following items:

Handheld Shower Head – This is a must! You need to be able to spray that water up there and really get it clean and fresh for the day.

White Washcloth – My favorite is BHG or Mainstay at Walmart. They are very inexpensive but are quality. They are not too thin or too thick, lather up well, are super soft, and dry fast. I like white washcloths so I can see everything. I know some of you may not look but I do because I want to know what is going on with my body and how much more I need to wash to feel squeaky clean.

Bar Soap or Body Wash – A cleansing bar soap or natural body wash with no toxins or parabens is the way to go. Choose one with a fruity scent that you can layer with a lotion to smell good all day. Look for one with built-in moisturizers so your skin won't be dry. Wash your body three times back to back and then rinse off with the handheld showerhead. Body wash is not for private parts.

vH Essentials Daily Feminine Wash – I use this because it contains non-toxic, natural, and organic ingredients like tea tree oil and prebiotics. It doesn't have garbage in it that will mess up my pH and has an odor-blocker vitamin blend for those times of the month. I use it every time I take a shower on my private parts only. A little goes a long way. Look up the ingredients list to make sure you aren't allergic to any of them, and don't use it if you are super sensitive. Wash down there at least twice in a row with only your fingers while counting backward from 30. Do not use a washcloth. Spray off the water and residue with the handheld showerhead. Use your fingers to smell to make sure it is gone. Trust me. You may think the faint smell of blood or bacteria is gone, but if you rush, it won't be. Don't scrub though. You're a delicate flower!

Scrub – A scrub is not just for a spa experience or bath. Exfoliating your skin of dead skin cells and softening rough spots is part of hygiene because it is necessary for clear and clean skin. If you don't exfoliate, the dead skin will sit on top of your skin and make it rough and look dull and dry. Scrubs also help before or after shaving or waxing. You should scrub your body two to three times a week.

Peroxide – This needs to be in a spray bottle like the ones you can find at Dollar Tree or the Beauty Supply store. Use peroxide when you are on your cycle and need something to make you feel even more fresh. It loosens and eliminates the smell of dried blood. You should shower daily and twice a day during the summer. Women have many things happen down there. We have our periods, urine, sweat, and discharge.

HANDS AND FEET

To stay clean and germ-free, wash your hands every time you use the bathroom, sneeze, play with pets, change your pad, or shake hands. You should scrub with warm water and soap for at least 15 seconds to keep clean hands and to prevent transmittable diseases. Keep hand sanitizer in your purse and use it if you can't get to water. Use a soapy nail brush to clean under your nails.

Keep your nails clean and your toenails trimmed and clean. A manicure is $10 and a pedicure is $20 at most nail salons, but you can give yourself one using the following steps, or you and a friend can give each other one:

1. Bowl with warm water and soap – Soak your hands in this and trim your cuticles.
2. Nail polish remover – Remove the old, beat-up polish that looks a mess.
3. Nail file and clipper – Trim your nails neat and pretty.

4. Polish and clear top coat – Put two coats of color and one top coat and let dry.

5. Lotion or hand/body oil – Oil your hands to keep them soft and moisturized.

MENSTRUAL CYCLE

I know the time of the month every girl feels her nastiest is when she is on her menstrual cycle. It's part of being a woman, but it doesn't mean you have to feel dirty or smelly. No one will even know if you're on if you follow these tips. While at school or work, have a small bag in your locker, book bag, or purse filled with the following so you will always be prepared:

1. Several organic sanitary napkins (I use L. brand from Target).

2. Organic baby wipes – Change your pad regularly and use the wipes to freshen up.

3. Extra pair of panties or period panties by Thinx.

4. A few small plastic sandwich bags to wrap pads in if you have to dispose of them at someone's house or walk out the stall at work or school with it. Wrap it in toilet paper and then put it in the baggy.

5. Small spray bottle with a mixture of peroxide and water (for accidents and blood stains).

TIPS TO SMELL GOOD ALL THE TIME

👑 Keep your hair and scalp clean.

👑 Shave or wax underarm and vagina hair so you won't sweat so much.

- ♛ Spray a nice, light perfume and walk through it. Put it behind your ears or lightly on your clothes. Don't drown yourself in it. That stinks even worse.
- ♛ Use a pillow and sheet spray.
- ♛ Use foot spray in your shoes to keep them fresh (especially gym shoes).
- ♛ Keep a perfumed sachet in your clothing drawer to keep clothes smelling fresh.
- ♛ Wear scented lotions.
- ♛ Carry mints for when you can't brush or floss after a meal.

Deodorant controls bacteria and adds a fragrance to your underarms. Antiperspirant stops or limits sweating. I use an organic deodorant without antiperspirant because antiperspirant causes many health risks in women. You may have to try a few deodorants until you find the one that works for you. I use Green Tidings from Amazon or Dove Zero Aluminum. It takes 7-10 days for your body to get used to natural deodorants, so don't give up. You won't sweat and stink forever.

PRAYER

Father, in the name of Jesus, I've heard the saying cleanliness is next to godliness. Well, I want to be clean and fresh at all times and be a good representative of Christ on the Earth. Help me to treat my body with tender loving care and help me avoid bad smells, disease, bacteria, colds, flus, or decay that will contribute to bad smells. Show me where I can take better care of myself from head to toe and forgive me for not taking care of my body the way I should have. Give me the time, strength, and energy to do what it takes to stay clean and present my body as a living sacrifice. Amen.

INTEGRITY

A good name is to be chosen rather than great riches, and favor is better than silver or gold. (Proverbs 22:1)

D o you know anyone who changes who they are depending on the day, crowd, or circumstance? Have you ever described somebody as fake or two-faced? Have you ever noticed that you feel like you have to compromise your actions based on the opportunity that presents itself? Integrity is being who you are no matter what and living by a certain moral code at all times, whether you are alone or not. The Bible tells us how important our name is. You should work hard to keep your name clean and pure so that when people hear it, they think of good things and not bad.

I don't know about you, but I don't want anyone to say, "I'm working with Tiffany on that project" and someone says, "Oh, she is underhanded and can't be trusted." I don't want to introduce myself and the person thinks to themselves, "Oh, I heard you're full of drama and always starting trouble." Of course, God gives us second chances and forgives, but people don't often forget. If any negative tea comes with your name, people will talk about it. Make sure they have positive things to say by walking with integrity.

Integrity not only means being honest but also making the right choices according to a moral standard or code. You must first have morals and they have to be important to you. It seems easy and like common sense to know right from wrong—don't steal, don't cheat, don't lie, don't gossip. The Bible says in 1 Corinthians 15:33 that "bad company corrupts good morals." Some people have been around wrong all their lives. They were raised by people who know the code but don't live by it, or they grew up in an environment that did people dirty as easy as breathing. They make excuses for these things because of a struggle or circumstance. These types of people will lead you the wrong way and stab you in the back. They know what to do but don't have it in them to do it. Stay away from those people. You may be headed down the right path, but when you start hanging with them, you'll start doing things you never thought you would do.

I have met people who swear they live by a code and would never fold on the people they care about, but then money, position, or a chance to get ahead comes along and they will sell their mama out. These people will burn you and make you regret ever meeting them because they are raised on survival and not love. They won't even feel bad about doing you or anyone else wrong because they feel like they have no other choice. They are only looking for where their next meal, dollar, or lick is coming from. They don't want to work hard or be held accountable. They just want to level up. These people never win long term, and you can't win with them.

When I lived in Chicago, I started mentoring two sisters. Their brother would come with them sometimes, and eventually, their cousins and friends came over too. I would teach them things, take them places, and show them a different way of life. Their mama seemed like she was trying hard to be the best mother she could be. She didn't have a job, had a GED, and got assistance from the state to take care of her children. Her children's father wasn't doing much, and I wanted to see her level up. Everyone who knows me knows I have a very big heart. Sometimes too big. When I see a need, I try my best to be the solution. We soon started calling each other sister, and I became like family to them. I celebrated birthdays, graduations, and was invited to all the cookouts. I did as much as I could to help the children and felt like I was making a difference in their lives.

One of my clients called me to travel out of town for a few months to run part of a project. I invited the kid's mama to come work with me so she could save the money she made to buy a car. She asked if she could bring her cousin along to work as well and I agreed. The first couple of days went smoothly. The excitement of being on the road and doing something different with their days made for some fun moments. The workers had no experience or education and agreed on how much they would be paid. The client showed up and saw that everything was going well and offered to double their pay, and they hadn't even started working yet! You may see that as a good thing, but these people had never made much money or even been on this type of project, and they saw dollar signs in the client.

Almost immediately, they started disrespecting and switching up on me. They no longer listened to my instructions and snapped at me when I asked them to do something. The girl's mama stopped wearing her uniform pants and started wearing pajama pants or holey leggings to work. She also stopped combing her hair. When I went to the client, instead of having my back, he took her side and eventually they all turned on me and left the housing we had for the project. The mama of the girls talked bad about me, and her cousin did the same and didn't even know me—all for some money. They thought if they turned him against me, they would be rewarded. They were wrong.

The client finally started seeing how lazy the girl I brought from Chicago was and fired her, and her cousin got so tired of the way he was spoken to by the client, he ended up calling me to apologize just before he quit. Their lack of integrity wasn't worth what they went through in the end, and they regretted doing me dirty. I never saw her or her cousin again. The children still reach out to me sometimes, and I continue to pray for them.

You can be kind and sweet to a person without integrity, but if all they have is the "gimme gimme, my name is Jimmy" mentality, they will only be nice to get what they want. It may look like they are getting away with living wild and doing what they want, but there are consequences for every action. The loss is always greater than the gain. You may not see them lose, and you may think they are doing better than you with their schemes and scams, but don't get it twisted—God will take care of them even if they did you wrong. You don't even have to lift a finger.

TRUTH VS. FAKE

Don't let anyone finesse you. Finesse means to trick. Some people lie as easily as they breathe. They can play a role like they are on a TV show! They'll work hard to lead you to believe anything if it gets them what they want. It is so important to recognize early in life the people who were raised in love and raised on survival. Most people raised in love value people over things. They know that the quality of the friendship or relationship outweighs what you can get from that person. When you live with integrity, you don't think with a scheming or scamming mindset, looking at what is in it for you and how you can come up off something. You see the value in hard work while praying to God for the wisdom to make decisions that will cause you to prosper without stealing from or cheating someone.

Pay close attention to how people move and talk when you meet them. You can tell a lot about a person's character by their conversation. People will tell on themselves and not even know it. People who don't have a real relationship with God may not even believe anything is wrong with using and scamming people. If they talk about partying, drinking, smoking, and sexing all the time instead of goals, dreams, and building, they may not know their worth or even have a vision for their lives. People with nothing to lose or nothing to live for will risk anything and certainly can't teach you anything except what not to do with your life. People who talk bad about their friends, family, and the people around them will do the same to you. People who sound like they are trying to convince or sell you something are likely shady. Don't trust these people. Don't hang around these people. Run fast, pray for them, and ask God to change their hearts.

〰〰〰〰〰〰〰〰〰〰〰〰〰〰〰〰〰〰〰〰〰〰〰

Don't be misled: No one makes a fool of God. What a person plants, he will harvest. The person who plants selfishness, ignoring the needs of others—ignoring God!—harvests a crop of weeds. All he'll have to show for his life is weeds! But the one who plants in response to God, letting God's Spirit do the growth work in him, harvests a crop of real life, eternal life. (Galatians 6:7-8)

〰〰〰〰〰〰〰〰〰〰〰〰〰〰〰〰〰〰〰〰〰〰〰

CONSEQUENCES

The foundation of a house is what keeps it from falling in. If you build your life on dishonesty, your life will crumble. Celebrities, politicians, and regular people will continue to try to hook and crook their way to wealth, riches, and fame and will continue to be exposed and paid back for the wrong they have done. It is not worth it, whether it is what people call a little white lie or a huge scamming operation. There are consequences to living a dishonest life. You may not even see it coming. You can get away with it for 15–20 years, but what is done in the dark will be brought to light. For instance, you may think you've gotten away with stealing or cheating, but if you plant seeds of dishonesty, it will grow in your life. You may meet a dishonest friend, work at a job with a dishonest boss, or be scammed by someone you trusted because of something you did in your past. Avoid this by doing what is right no matter how hard or inconvenient. You'll feel better about yourself when you've done things the right way.

INTEGRITY IS BEAUTIFUL

Surround yourself with people who sharpen you and make you better, not worse—people who check you when you have lost your way. You can't put on and take off integrity like a coat. It has to be in your heart to do the right thing no matter what. You can be smart, pretty, and popular, but if you don't have integrity, your blessings won't last. You will fail every time, your reputation won't survive it, and you will be exposed and humiliated. This isn't to scare you or make you feel paranoid, but it is to drive home how important it is to choose right over wrong. Choose good over bad. Ask God to help you if your judgment is off or if you are around people who make you feel that doing dishonest things are a way of life.

Ill-gotten treasures have no lasting value, but righteousness delivers from death. (Proverbs 10:2)

Don't allow yourself any room to live without integrity. I know you want nice things and to live like the people you see on TV or social media, with name brands, nice cars, and big mansions, but you'll be proud of yourself when you accomplish your goals the right way. Dishonesty is not only a character flaw but becomes a bad habit, and bad habits grow. It can start off small, like when a cashier gives you too much change at the register. If you notice, give it back. Or when you are too tired to do a paper for school, don't go online and start copying and pasting from different sites to get it over with. Manage your time right so you won't have to steal and cheat to pass a class.

When you do things like this and get away with it, you will start to believe it is okay, and next thing you know, you will find a wallet on the ground and keep the money. You feel lucky or make excuses like "finders keepers, losers weepers," and then eventually, you are looking for ways to level up without working. It is a very slippery slope. You don't have to live like that. I've said it before and I'll say it again: God has already given you everything you need to be what you were born to be and have what you were created to have. Do things His way and watch the blessings flow.

Even if you weren't taught as a little girl to be honest, you can still choose to tell the truth at all times and live right today. Some people believe as long as you don't get caught or nobody gets hurt, you can do whatever you want. Sure, you may get away with cheating on a test, stealing clothes from the store, lying about where you are or what you're doing on social media, or even talking about your friend behind her back. However, the bad seeds you plant will sprout up bad fruit and come back to bite you. Make sure you plant good seeds so you can reap good fruit.

A young woman with integrity is beautiful not only in the eyes of God but everyone around her. When you are dependable, trustworthy, have a good reputation, and choose to do the right thing, you will be honored, cherished, and treated with respect. Your name will be like a diamond that shines in the light and will attract the right things and people to your life. Let your actions be honorable and honest. You will sleep well at night and look in the mirror with pride and not shame. Always remember, the choices you make with integrity today create a successful, lasting life for you tomorrow.

I know it is not always easy to make the right choice and do things the hard way instead of the easy way, but the time, effort, and energy you put in to create your success with integrity will make you stronger, wiser, and happier in the long term.

PRAYER

Father, in the name of Jesus, thank you for your love, guidance, and patience as I develop into the young woman you created me to be. Please continue to give me the strength to resist the pressure that comes from all directions to do things that are opposed to your Word and will. Help me to always choose the way of integrity and allow my life to be a shining example. Amen.

J O Y

Be cheerful no matter what; pray all the time; thank God no matter what happens. This is the way God wants you who belong to Christ Jesus to live.
(1 Thessalonians 16:18)

Lately, everyone is talking about Living Your Best Life. When Oprah coined the phrase, it meant that in every area of your life, you are reaching your full potential. Fast forward and Lil Duval made a song with the same title, and the lyrics are about making the best of every situation you're faced with and not arguing with anybody trying to bring you down. What nobody tells you is how to live your best life for real.

I believe one of the major keys to having a fulfilled life is joy. Joy in the dictionary means "a feeling of great pleasure or happiness," but the joy the Bible wants us to have is so much more. It took me some time to study and learn what joy was, and I found that it is not just a temporary feeling you get when something good happens. Feelings are not reliable because they can change from minute to minute. Joy is always there to help you through hard times. Feelings come from life's ups and downs. Joy lifts you up and holds you down. It is like a superpower.

For example, a teacher at school has been doing the most. She always calls you to the board, grades your papers unfairly, and it seems like she has something against you. You dread going to her class and would rather stay home. Instead of faking sick, you talk to a trusted friend, pray with them about the issue, and go into the classroom knowing God will work it out. The next time you are called to the board, you go up there and handle your business with a smile. Someone without joy would let this bother them all year, but you have joy. Joy doesn't make the problem go away, but it makes the problem seem like no big deal. Let's find out why and how to get some.

> **My brethren, count it all joy when you fall into various trials, knowing that the testing of your faith produces patience. (James 1:2-3)**

God wants you to "count it all joy" when things happen in your life. When you do this, you will mature, get stronger, and be better off. If things are crazy at home, your friend is acting funny, you're struggling to focus in school, and you don't feel like yourself, know that these things are only temporary, and you'll come out better on the other end of the struggle. You can find joy in that. When you remember that God will take care of you through it all and that he has a plan for you, you can hold on to joy during your hard times. When you finish going through the pain, sadness, sickness, or drama and have gotten over it, you can help someone else by encouraging and supporting them. Once you see what you've overcome, you'll realize you are a better and stronger person. When you win, you can cause someone else to win and find joy in that too.

Joy is a state of mind that starts from within. It is different from happiness because it has nothing to do with what is going on in your life. Happiness is temporary and doesn't last long. Joy is forever. Happiness comes from people, material things, good news, and special events. When you get an A on your test, a friend comes to visit you, or you get a new pair of shoes, you are happy about it. However, it wears off, and by the time next week comes, you're looking for something else to give you that feeling. If the opposite of these things happens, like you fail a test, your favorite pair of shoes gets messed up, or your best friend moves away, then you'd be unhappy. Even if you had a great day and felt happy, something could easily change your mood. It's nice to be happy, but it's not enough. You need the constant flow of positive thinking that joy brings.

Joy is a gift from God. The wonderful thing is that it is always there whether you are having a bad day, week, month, or year! Joy ONLY comes from God, and it is much deeper than happiness. It is one of the fruit of the spirit, and every Christian should have it. It's important for you as a young lady growing into a woman to have joy because it will prepare you for life's challenges. I wish someone had warned me that life would not always be about music videos, cute clothes, and amusement parks. I would have been more ready emotionally for rough times because they are a part of life.

I started working at the White House at 16 years old. I was so young and still in high school but wore suits and heels and carried a briefcase like I was grown. I was raised in the church, but just like now, not many programs prepare young people for real life. I was a young girl in a grown-up world. By 17, I had my first cell phone, college tuition, a car note, full-time job, a full class load, and no clue what I was doing emotionally. School and my Work-Study program prepared me for the job and college, but nothing prepared me for real life. It was what we call a rude awakening.

At that time, I thought all I needed to know was how to file papers in alphabetical order, type letters, and answer phones. Yes, I needed those things to get paid, but no one ever sat me down and said, "Okay, you may have managers or coworkers who don't know how to talk to you; you may feel overwhelmed with school and work; you need to pay your bills on time or something will get cut off." I had to learn as I went along. I'm thankful I had a strong foundation by growing up in church, but even that wasn't enough. I didn't have a real relationship with God yet, and the only thing I knew about joy was that it was my favorite cousin's name.

Prayerfully, this book gives you the jewels that school or others haven't. I'm here to tell you now, little sister, life can be hard. Sometimes it will feel crazy, scary, and impossible, and sometimes it will feel like all three at the same time. You may not get every job you apply for. You may be rejected and betrayed sometimes. You may get your heart broken. Some days you will feel stupid, ugly, or both. Some days you will feel alone even if you're not. Sometimes you will be sad and cry all day. Sometimes you will be disappointed in yourself. Life will be a rollercoaster. But spoiler alert, you will survive and, with joy, you will thrive!

I was so shocked when my heart got broken for the first time. I didn't know it would feel like my head was spinning and my heart had been crushed in a blender and then poured into a glass of fire. I didn't know I would stay up for hours at night asking myself what I did to deserve this or if the pain would ever get better. After the second time getting my heart broken, I knew Jesus. I had such a strong relationship with Him that I didn't lose my mind when the man I loved chose to disappear and never call again instead of telling me what was going on in his life.

Yes, it still hurt so bad that I felt like I had been pushed off a cliff and fell hard on my butt. Yes, I still woke up at the same time every night that he used to call me when he got off his night job. And yes, I still blamed myself in many ways; however, the difference was I never lost my joy. I held my head up high; didn't turn to things like drugs, food, sex, and alcohol to soothe my pain; and knew God would heal my broken heart and bless me with the man He created for me. I stayed focused on my projects, prayed like never before, and encouraged myself.

I knew that even if I made a mistake and chose the wrong person to trust, God is a God of second chances. Most importantly, I knew that before I was even born, God mapped out a beautiful, adventurous, and purposeful life for me. I knew when the pain was gone and my heart was healed, I would still have that same life but be wiser, stronger, and more cautious next time.

That is where joy comes in. It helps you keep what is important at the front of your heart and mind so you won't go off the deep end in troubled times. Joy has many other benefits. A study I read on Medical Daily's website found that people who walk in joy are healthier and live longer and don't get sick as much. Stress has a negative effect on your body, and when you keep a joyful spirit, you have less stress.

WHAT BRINGS YOU JOY?

So how do you keep a joyful spirit? Well, first, you should make a list. This is the key to making sure you have the tools you need to succeed in every area. It is important to know what brings you joy, not what makes you happy, because you learned that happiness is temporary. I love shopping, but I wouldn't write it down because once I am done shopping and the clothes are hanging in my closet, the excitement is gone. I don't feel it again until I either go shopping again or I wear the outfit, and even that lasts for a few minutes. Joy keeps going.

So write down things that will fill your heart up and give you a smile that no one and nothing can take off your face. My Joy List includes places, people, and activities. My nieces and nephews bring me so much joy. I love spending time with them, doing things for them, and watching them grow up and get smarter every day. No matter what is going on, if I even think of them, I smile and my heart feels full. When I see them smile and hear them call me auntie or even when they text me how good they did on a report card, I feel like I can go on no matter what is bothering me.

Another example is the beach. I love water! Growing up in Maryland and Washington DC, I was always close to the water, and then I moved to Chicago and lived right around the corner from the beach for years. I love to travel to the Caribbean to lay there and soak up the sun. Just the thought of the warm, soft sand, the smell and peaceful sounds of the water, and sipping a virgin pina colada puts my problems at the back of my mind and God's unlimited grace at the front. Other things include:

👑 Doing my Queen Connection workshops for girls 12–21
👑 Planning events

👑 Worshipping God

👑 Traveling

👑 Helping others achieve their goals

Your list doesn't have to be long, but once you finish it, keep those things, people, and activities as part of your normal routine to keep your joy flowing.

So if there is any encouragement in Christ, any comfort from love, any participation in the Spirit, any affection and sympathy, complete my joy by being of the same mind, having the same love, being in full accord and of one mind. (Philippians 2:1-2)

GET A JOYFRIEND

Everyone needs a JoyFriend before they even think about having a boyfriend. Sometimes when I am sad, I call someone who will let me be sad and cry and they will just listen. Once I vent, I'm okay and the friend has served their purpose. It can be about something small like missing my family since I'm in Atlanta away from everyone I know and love, but once I get it out, I'm good.

Other times when I'm mad, I want to call someone who will be mad right along with me so we can both fuss. This friend will even ask if I need her to pull up on somebody just to make sure I'm good. This is that ride or die friend who is ready to defend you at all costs. By the way, pulling up on anyone in this crazy world is certainly not a good idea, but it is always nice to have someone who is willing and ready.

Most times I need a JoyFriend. My aunt Patty and I are super close. We talk almost every day and sometimes for hours at a time, and it is never a waste of time. She is super strong, super smart, and the most encouraging person I know. Even when she has her own issues, she pushes those aside to talk to me. When I hang up the phone with her, I feel like I can accomplish anything. She never lets me stay in a funk. Yes, she listens, but she points out when how I am feeling is becoming a habit and reminds me of why I am here and that what I'm going through has a purpose. She also reminds me that God is in control and has my back. She prays for me, and when the issue is serious, she recruits others to pray for me. She is my JoyFriend through and through. Get you a Joy-Friend and be one for someone else.

> **You make known to me the path of life; in your presence there is fullness of joy; at your right hand are pleasures forevermore. (Psalms 16:11)**

WORSHIP

Every day, you should strive to be in God's presence. God is bigger than any problem you have, and He has made a way for you to connect with Him on a very deep level. You do this through worship. You don't have to wait until Sunday service to feel God's presence. He can be with you everywhere you go; even your bedroom, the park, your car, or the beach can be a perfect place to worship and get filled with His joy.

To get in His presence, turn the television off and put your phone down unless you're playing worship music to push you deeper into the presence of the Lord. Start telling God who He is to you. He is your comforter, provider, best friend, and Father. He is faithful, worthy, awesome, mighty, and strong. The list goes on and on. Tell Him "Thank You, Lord, Hallelujah, I Worship You" over and over. Who is God to you? Write it down and let Him know every chance you get.

Set a timer to worship for at least 10 minutes a day. You'll start to get the hang of it, and you'll feel a sense of peace and joy and love wash over you. Your problems will seem smaller and your God will definitely be bigger. Don't go a day without worship, especially when you need to get filled with the gifts and the fruit of the Spirit. I guarantee you'll feel on top of the world and like you can accomplish and overcome anything that comes at you.

Don't be dejected and sad, for the joy of the Lord is your strength! (Nehemiah 8:10b)

READ AND SPEAK THE WORD

Don't you want to be strong? I don't know if anyone has ever told you, but the real you is a spirit that lives in a body. Just like you should work out to strengthen and keep your body moving and healthy, you should do the same thing for your spirit. Instead of weights and machines, you use your Bible to build yourself up. God's Word gives you understanding, wisdom, and everything you need to live a good life full of joy, peace, strength, and love. Whatever you are going through, look up the subject on Google and dig into the Scripture by looking up every word in the concordance and a dictionary so you know what it means. A concordance is a Bible study tool that gives you the Greek and Hebrew definition of a word and helps you understand the Scriptures better.

Read the New Living Translation or the Message to see a breakdown of the verse in plainer English. The Scriptures that speak out to you are the ones you should recite and write as many times as possible to remember and get in your spirit. That way when an issue comes up, the Word is buried in your heart and the joy that is already there is instantly activated.

SING

God loves when you sing to Him. When you have joy, you rejoice. It's as simple as that. One way of rejoicing is through singing. Put a song in your heart that makes you feel even stronger and gives you hope and watch your joy overflow. Some of my favorite songs to sing to myself throughout the day about joy are "Joyful, Joyful" (made popular by the movie *Sister Act*) and "Oh Lord, How Excellent" by Richard Smallwood. What songs give you hope when you feel down?

PRAYER

Father, in the name of Jesus, thank you for this teaching on the importance of joy. Thank you for giving me the gift of joy and allowing it to always be there when I need it. Help me to always look to you for whatever I need. I am thankful that the world didn't give me joy and the world can't take it away. Remind me to worship you, sing songs of joy, and read your Word regularly so I may cause a constant flow of joy that will help me overcome the issues that come with living life. I give all my worries to you and trade them for your unspeakable joy. Fill me with your joy and take away any sadness, struggle, or stress in Jesus' name. Amen.

KNOWLEDGE

*The fear of the LORD is the beginning of knowledge,
but fools despise wisdom and instruction.
(Proverbs 1:7)*

Queens chase nothing except God, her purpose, and knowledge. Queens don't even chase money. When you chase purpose, the money comes. When you chase God, your blessings, protection, and wisdom will flow. When you chase knowledge, you'll have more power and the keys to anything you are trying to accomplish. The Bible says in Hosea 4:6, "My people are destroyed for a lack of knowledge." Destroy means to be damaged and ruined. That may mean spiritual, mental, or physical damage. If you don't know anything, you can't do anything. This means you should fill your mind with the right knowledge so you can have the right results. You should never watch more reality TV and junk TV than you do things that will feed you knowledge. You should grow your vocabulary by learning one new word a week. Curse words should never be part of your vocabulary. Slang should only be used in casual situations. If you want to be successful, respected, and the best at what you do, you must not only be knowledgeable but sound knowledgeable.

Thank God for Wi-Fi and Google. When I was a teenager, we had to pay for each minute of dial-up internet through an old company called AOL. It would use your phone line to connect, and if someone called while it was connected, you would lose the connection and have to start all over again. When I had a paper due, I had to use an encyclopedia. They were huge books in alphabetical order that told the history of a subject. By the time some of my papers were due, that information was outdated or incomplete.

Now you can go online and type in any question and Google will come back with several pages of results and answers to your questions, including videos. I love this because I am always trying to learn something, no matter how random. If someone uses a word I don't know, I immediately Google it to find out what it means, how it's spelled, and how to use it, and then I include it in my vocabulary. If I am hungry and have a taste for something, I can enter in the ingredients I want to cook with and find a recipe or video to show me what to make. If I want to know the deeper meaning of a subject, I study it with videos and articles until I understand it. Doing these things keeps my mind sharp, helps me grow my companies, and gives me an edge over most people because most they don't read on a regular basis.

Most people would rather Snapchat all day, scroll down their timelines, watch reality television, play games on their phone, and waste time doing things that don't matter. You can't get that far doing this day after day, year after year. The last place you want to be 365 days from now is in the same place. When you have dreams and a plan, you must go after it by increasing your knowledge. Now is the time to choose to do different things than everyone else if you want to be different and live differently.

Study to shew thyself approved unto God, a workman that needeth not to be ashamed, rightly dividing the word of truth. (2 Timothy 2:15)

STUDY, READ, WATCH, AND LISTEN

Your brain is a muscle. Reading exercises it to keep it strong. Every successful person reads. You must know what is going on around you. God has given you talents, but you have to know what the problems are to make solutions. Those solutions may be tied to your purpose and will help people. Read at least one book a month. I still find time to do this no matter how busy I get. When I was younger, I used to read one book a week trying to learn as much as possible. I am not talking about love stories or mystery novels. Those are fun to read and help you escape, but I am talking about subjects that will make you a better person, give you new information, and increase your knowledge.

Queens who read regularly usually have a great vocabulary. I know when you text your friends, everything is all emojis and letters that mean certain words, but that won't work in the real world. When you're sending an email, writing a book, or expressing yourself in school, you'll need to know the proper terms to use. People who chase knowledge know that when someone's loved one passes, it's "sorry for your loss" not "sorry for your lost." When you know the difference between "there, their, and they're," people can take you more seriously. When you use the right "two, too, or to," your email won't be deleted as soon as someone gets your resume. Study these things and make sure you're learning a new word every day.

You all have it easier than I did. YouTube and audiobooks allow you to multitask. You don't always have to dive into a book to learn. You can listen to a book in the author's voice while cleaning your room and have a video playing while doing your hair or driving. Watch documentaries, listen to TedTalks on a subject, and always listen to the Word. You build yourself up when you listen to preachers and teachers, and this helps build your faith as well. You should also study the Bible so you can lead others to Christ, know how to deal with practical and spiritual issues, and follow the instructions God has given you.

EXPAND YOUR CIRCLE

Hang with people who know more than you. Right now, you may be the smartest one in your circle. I'm sorry, but that is not a good thing long term. Start looking outside of your circle of friends and family so you can get to the next level of knowledge. If you are in school and notice someone is better at a subject than you, start talking to that person. That doesn't mean trust them with your business or let them in on your deepest feelings. It means to talk to them so you can learn more.

If you are interested in a certain hobby or have a certain talent, seek out the best people in your city who do what you do or want to do. See if they are teaching classes, see if they will give you some tips, or get permission to watch them do what they do so you can learn more. The people who are where you want to be can help motivate and stretch you. They may even agree to mentor you. This is called networking, which will help you grow your circle of people. I didn't say circle of friends.

That is a mistake many people make. They think because they have one goal or subject in common with someone they meet through networking that they should be friends. That is not the purpose of networking. I said circle of people who will help you increase your knowledge, so be careful. Don't share everything with these people. Just ask questions, observe, and gain the information you need to succeed.

EXPERIENCE IS KEY

If you have studied, watched videos, and talked to people about what you are trying to learn, now it is time to gain knowledge through experience. Research internships or jobs in your field of study. If your goal is to become a salon owner, find the best salon in your area that has good reviews, a valid license, and does the hairstyles you want. Get a few letters of recommendation from teachers or other adults who know you and your character and include them with your resume. If you have no job history, include classes you have taken, videos you've watched, or even years of chores you've done at home to show your level of experience.

Call the salon and ask for the owner and request the time he or she is available to speak with you in person about an internship. If they are not hiring, don't beg for a paid position. Put your paperwork in a folder and at the set time, go introduce yourself and offer services such as organization, cleaning bathrooms, greeting customers, washing and folding towels, or sweeping and mopping floors. Tell the owner what your goals are. People like to give back and help young people. Do what you have to do until you get where you want to go. This experience will not only look good on your resume and teach you discipline, time management, and customer service, but it will increase your knowledge about entrepreneurship, customer service, and salon management. You can use this same plan and apply it to whatever you are interested in doing. Don't let anything stop you from gaining more knowledge through experience. School will never be enough. I know many people who graduate from high school and college and because all they have is a degree, people with more experience and knowledge are chosen over them.

PRAY

When you pray, you don't just talk to God about what you want Him to do for you. You also listen. It's a conversation. Imagine if your friend called you, ran her mouth, asked you for a bunch of stuff, and then hung up on you. That is what you do when you don't spend time listening to God. You should set time aside to sit quietly and listen for instruction and information. The knowledge you get from God will help you with your dreams, goals, and life in general. Allow nothing to hinder your prayer life. Set aside time each morning and night to talk to God about what you should do to gain more knowledge and get closer to fulfilling your purpose. Remember, the main reason you were even born is to fulfill your purpose. It makes perfect sense to ask the One who gave you your purpose for guidance.

HEARING FROM GOD

God is speaking all the time. It is important to put the phone away, turn off the television and radio, and sit quietly on a daily basis to hear His voice. The way you know you are hearing from God is to test what you believe you are hearing with the Word. The Word is His will, and He will never tell you to do something that isn't part of His will. If what you believe you are hearing is positive, true, and righteous, chances are the instruction is from God. You get to know His voice the more time you spend with Him and fill yourself up with the things of God.

PRAYER

Father, in the name of Jesus, thank you for the ability to get knowledge in so many ways. Take any laziness away from me and replace it with a thirst for knowledge. I want to be who you made me to be. Help me network with the right people and block the wrong people with wrong motives from coming into my life. Send me a mentor, Lord, who will pour into me and help me on my path to fulfilling your purpose for me.

L O V E

1 Corinthians 13:13 - Three things will last forever–faith, hope, and love–and the greatest of these is LOVE.

We hear about the word love on a daily basis in songs, on television, in books, and even from people, but do we really know what it is and what real love looks like? I want you to be able to distinguish real love from fake love so you can avoid the heartbreak and pain I have suffered. If you are a very loving person, sometimes people will see that and try to take advantage of it. It is important to be able to recognize the signs of real love so you can know how to receive and give it.

You can give all your clothes away to charity, help people with their homework, feed the homeless, and remember every Scripture, but if you do not have love, the Bible says it doesn't matter and you're useless. I'm on a path to show everyone I meet the kind of love that God wants me to have. Whether it is a family member, someone I meet at the store, or someone who cut me off in traffic, I want to have a strong love walk. God is love, and if He lives in us, people should experience love when they meet us.

The Bible talks about different types of love, but I won't get into that here. I'm going to talk about the God kind of love, which 1 Corinthians 13 describes. When you got to this chapter, you probably thought about the love from a guy in your life or a future husband, but God's love is the only love you should actively seek. Self-love is the next love you should work to have every single day. If you don't love yourself, you won't even know how to love anyone else and will accept any old low-level, funky treatment that may look and sound like love but will be as fake as a $3 bill.

You'll have plenty of time to experience love with a boy. I know it is exciting and feels great to have those butterflies in your stomach and get those cute texts saying, "Good morning, beautiful" with emoji hearts. I know you want to take selfies together and post them on social media and have inside jokes between you and him. However, if I could go back in time, the last thing I'd do is get in a relationship with anyone before I turned 21. I would have focused more on school and work and building a strong foundation for myself. It is rare that the boy you talk to in your teens is the one you will stay with forever. It is rare that someone won't get hurt, and it is even more rare that a teenage relationship won't distract you from your goals and dreams. As a teen, you don't know what real love is. Yes, you'll have the feeling, but you won't have the knowledge to make it work, and love is more than a feeling. Once you realize the feeling is all you had, you'll see it isn't worth what you may have lost.

You may lose time, which you never get back and could have used to be productive. You may lose some nights of sleep and get heartbroken. And last but certainly not least, you may lose your virginity, which is the last thing you want to lose. You can't get it back and should make sure that who you give it to actually earned it. Save yourself for marriage and your life will be a whole lot easier. You are worth the wait, and I promise most of the boys you meet at this age are not worth your time, virginity, or energy.

I met my first real teenage boyfriend at 15. I thought it was real love because he would give me compliments and kiss me like in the movies right outside of church. I thought I was living on the edge. I would skip school for him, ride a bus and train to get to his Northeast neighborhood in Washington, DC, and hang out with him all day making goo-goo eyes and looking dumb as a mug. I didn't love myself enough to know that school should have been my priority, so I did whatever he asked me to do. All I thought I knew at 15 was that I loved him and that we were going to get married and have cute chocolate babies. Looking back, all I really knew was how to be a big idiot for a guy who couldn't even afford to take me on a real date.

My stupidity was cut short when, during the interview period for my White House job, I was called in for a special meeting. I was so nervous when I walked through the gate, showed my ID to the guard, and waited for them to allow me through the metal detectors. I almost peed on myself when they showed me his mug shots and told me he steals cars and sells drugs and that I couldn't get the job if they caught me with him again. He was the one who drove me to the White House that day for my meeting!

After I swallowed the lump in my throat and held back scary tears, I promised them I would never see him again, and I meant it. My mama would have killed me if she found out I lost a job because I was seeing a criminal behind her back. When I walked out of the building, I looked to the left and saw him sitting in a blue car that was probably stolen. Instead, I walked to the right and to the train station. I called him when I got home and told him it was over for good. I may not have known how to love myself back then, but I definitely knew that the little puppy love I had for him wasn't worth my future, so I let him go.

AGAPE – THE GOD KIND OF LOVE

The highest form of love is known as Agape—the God kind of love, which is unconditional, stands the test of time, and is 100% selfless. It is all about "what can I do for you?" instead of "what can you do for me?" regardless of the circumstances. It gives no matter what, even if it doesn't get anything back. We should all strive for this type of love to have the strongest friendships and relationships. This is the type of LOVE the world needs to see the God in us so that they may be drawn to Him.

For God so loved the world that he gave his one and only Son, that whoever believes in him shall not perish but have eternal life (John 3:16). Because Adam sinned, God knew we would be punished forever if He did not send His son to die for our sins. We did nothing to deserve it or earn it, and sometimes we forget just how much He loves us, but He does it anyway. The Bible says that nothing can separate us from the love of God. Jesus' life was the ultimate sacrifice and display of love, and we should look to that sacrifice daily and apply the principle to our actions and words in order to be an example of God in the Earth.

The true definition of agape love is found in 1 Corinthians 13:4-8. I am giving you the Message translation because it breaks it all the way down. All the things below have nothing to do with feelings and everything to do with action. Love is an action word like run, jump, or dance. You can't do these things without action. So if someone tells you they love you but isn't showing you the things listed below, its fake. The passage says:

Love never gives up. God doesn't give up on us, so when someone does you wrong or annoys you, give them a chance to make things right and ask for forgiveness. If they continue doing these things, you are not wrong to stay away from them. Don't be foolish and keep giving them chances to disrespect you, but don't give up if they make a mistake. Hurt people hurt people. Some people you will come across are messed up from the things that have happened to them. You never know what not giving up on them will do for them; however, use wisdom and take everything to God in prayer. Sometimes not giving up just means praying for them and loving them from a distance. It definitely doesn't mean being used or abused in any way.

Love cares more for others than for self. You can't be selfish and say you love someone. Love is about giving, not getting. Give a kind word, give a word of encouragement, give a hug, give a smile, give your time, energy, and effort. But the important thing is that it must come from your heart. Don't do it just to say you are doing it. Be kind and selfless because it is the right thing to do and because of the love of God flowing through you. You can tell when you are not spending time with God enough if you don't have and give love for others. Time with Him refills you so that you have more to give. Pay attention to when you feel drained and empty. There is plenty more in store for you when you spend time in prayer and worship.

Love doesn't want what it doesn't have. Be happy with what God has blessed you with. Don't look at someone else's blessing and get upset. God will make things happen for you that he made JUST for you. Don't be jealous or start hating on somebody because they seem more blessed than you. The person you are looking at with designer clothes or a nice new car or a nice hairstyle may be struggling in other areas. I know people who have all of the latest designer shoes and clothes and the nicest cars that are not happy, take pills to sleep at night, and can't get along with everyone. Looks can be deceiving. Don't allow that hate to grow in your heart for what you think they have that you don't or you'll block your own blessings. Celebrate when your family and friends have good news. Your time is coming.

Love doesn't strut, doesn't have a swelled head, doesn't force itself on others, isn't always me first. Sometimes you gotta chill. Love is very patient and understanding. If someone doesn't feel like being bothered or is acting funny, don't trip. Love doesn't walk in pride, which means you can't think you know everything and talk down to others. That is not love. Don't ever look down on someone. That is not love, and God will humble you quickly if you start treating people like they are beneath you. Always remember where you came from and be sweet and nice to others.

Doesn't fly off the handle. Watch your temper and your mouth. I used to pride myself on cussing somebody out to the fullest extent of the law! I loved how stupid they would look when I went off and put them in their place. The last time I did it after I committed myself to live right, I felt so bad and actually apologized. I cried and asked God's forgiveness because I know I am supposed to be an example and to walk in love no matter what. People are always going to try you and challenge you and even cuss you out for no reason. You are royalty and do not have to come off your throne to stoop to their level. Even if it hurts, don't get even, get to praying and give it to God.

Doesn't keep score of the sins of others. God is very forgiving, and as He forgives, so should you. You can't get His forgiveness if you don't forgive others. That is how it works. I know if you are hurt, you want to see them hurt, but it is better to just leave them alone. They will miss you when you're gone, and even if they don't, it is better to leave it in the past and stop rehearsing what they did. You can't heal nor can you properly forgive and move on when you keep bringing up what they did. Chances are they don't even care enough to feel bad, so move on and let it go.

It is never glad about injustice but rejoices whenever truth wins out. You should always tell the truth no matter what. We talked about integrity and how important it is to be honest and upfront with people. This shows love in a major way and causes you to be trustworthy. Love is pure like the truth, so if you say you love someone, you act in purity and truth.

Puts up with anything. Allow the love of God to flow through you so that you never clap back and you cover your friends and family. Don't tell their business, don't gossip about them, and always have their back. That is what love is. Recently, a family member hurt me so bad with their words. It doesn't change my love for them, but it does change the way I deal with them. I had to set boundaries to guard my heart, but I still wish them the best, and if they desperately needed me, I'd be there for them. God is the same way with you. No matter what you do, nothing can make him stop loving you even when you act up.

Trusts God always. God is the ultimate example of love and will always show you the way to improve your love walk if you let Him. Trust in Him and believe that He has your back. When friends and family turn their back on you or betray you, trust God to make it right. A woman who is like my second mother always tells me, "God ain't sleep!" and my grandmother always said, "The Lord sits high and He looks low." Those two taught me that God is always watching, and He sees what is happening. Even if it feels like others have forgotten you or have done you dirty, God is there and can fix it.

Always looks for the best, never looks back, but keeps going to the end. Love never dies. Real love overcomes everything. It's important to check your love walk using the above definitions as well as ask family and friends how they think you're doing. You want to make sure your love looks like the God kind of love. You want to be known for how loving you are. I didn't use to have a big heart but I've been described as having a "heart of a giant or a heart of gold" because every day I genuinely try to be a good person who exhibits the love of Jesus even when it is hard to love.

Like I've said before, we are spiritual beings who have a soul (mind, will, and emotions) and live in a body. Agape love, the highest form of love, is spiritual. You can only experience it when you tap into God's love for you. You can tell a lot about someone by the way that they "love." If it is all about them, it is not love. If it throws your past in your face, it is not love. If it uses or abuses you, it is not love. If it only cares about what they can get from you, it is not love. If a guy or a girl does not know God, they do not know what real love is, so be very careful of allowing people into your life who have no foundation in God. They almost always will hurt or disappoint you. Do not expect anything from anyone who doesn't have a relationship with God. The love He has is so strong and so powerful it can change even the meanest person.

> *For I am convinced that neither death nor life, neither angels nor demons, neither the present nor the future, nor any powers, neither height nor depth, nor anything else in all creation, will be able to separate us from the love of God that is in Christ Jesus our Lord. (Romans 8:37)*

It is important to know what your love language is. Gary Chapman's book, *The 5 Love Languages,* will help you know the way you receive love so you can recognize what you need from your friends and family.

PRAYER

Father, in the name of Jesus, thank you for your love that lasts forever. I am so grateful that no matter the mistakes I make, you will forgive me and continue to love me. I thank you for teaching me the different kinds of love. Help me to be able to tell which kind of love I am being given and to avoid the distractions and traps Satan has set up to take me off my path. Help me to walk in agape love so that others can see me as an example of you in the earth and be encouraged. Help me to stay patient, kind, selfless, and forgiving in Jesus' name. Amen.

MODESTY

Do not allow this world to mold you in its own image. Instead, be transformed from the inside out by renewing your mind. As a result, you will be able to discern what God wills and whatever God finds good, pleasing, and complete. (Romans 12:2)

*J*know this word sounds old-fashioned, and it isn't spoken of much in this world of Hot Girls, Slut Walks, and IG models that promote girls showing off their bodies to the world, wearing thongs in public, getting "flewed out," and twerking all over the place. Modesty, in a word, means decency. I know that everything you see on television, social media, and in the world points in the opposite direction, but Queens are called to a higher standard of living. Being an example is part of your purpose so that younger girls can model your behavior, dress, and speech and boys and men will treat you with the utmost respect.

1 Timothy 2:9 says *"that women should adorn themselves in respectable apparel, with modesty and self-control."* This means you should avoid clothing that reveals too much skin or your private parts. You are called to represent God on the earth, and when people look at you, you should think about your image. You can't expect people to receive from you if you are dressed just like the world, and you certainly can't expect respect if you talk and act like the world.

> **You shall be a crown of beauty in the hand of the Lord. (Isaiah 62:3)**

When you know your worth, you respect yourself and understand that you are royalty. You are a princess, and your Father God is your King. Your life is your throne, and the daily decisions you make will build your throne. Do you want your throne to be built on righteousness or ratchetness? Living a righteous and modest life won't be perfect or easy, but you will get more respect from others and people will take you more seriously. Living a ratchet and immodest lifestyle may be wild and fun sometimes; however, it will be hard for people to look at you as more than just a good-time girl. That doesn't mean you have to dress like a nun and stay in the house all the time; it just means you put extra thought into the way you present yourself to the world.

Good and godly guys do not want to wife someone who has shown all her goods to everyone who clicks on her social media page. They are created to chase and hunt. You should dress the way you want to be addressed and leave things to the imagination. If you wear clothes fit for someone on a stripper pole, you won't attract men who want to stick around. They may seem like they are chasing you, but they will only be after one thing. Now being modest doesn't mean you have to walk around wearing a choir robe, but you definitely shouldn't leave the house looking like you are about to audition for an All-Star Twerk team. I know it is fun to dance to your favorite song, but it shouldn't be done on a platform that can come back to haunt you when it is time for an interview or background check. Save it for your husband. A godly guy with good principles and morals will not want to claim someone who shows their assets off so easily. A boy will use you up, show you off, and even seem proud to walk beside you, but a good and godly man wants his wife to be modest. What you wear is an invitation. Who and what are you inviting?

Another tip to display modesty is to watch your eye contact. You don't have to look down at the ground, but when you meet a guy, whether it is someone who is interested in you, a teacher, a pastor, someone at church, or even your friend's boyfriend, don't look him dead in the eye. It can come off flirtatious, like you are being too forward. Modesty is simply about being ladylike. Being modest means you don't wear booty shorts and skirts with half your butt cheeks out. Being modest means you don't wear low-cut blouses, see-through shirts or no bra with your nipples and boobs for everyone to see. Being modest means you watch your speech, refrain from using curse words and sexual talk, and don't allow gossip to leave your lips. Being modest means you don't send "sexts" and naked pictures and videos of yourself to boys/men. If a guy asks you to send him a picture, do like LeToya Luckett did—send a picture of your elbow or your big toe.

Being modest will set an example for the people who weren't taught how to dress and act like a lady. I know it sounds restrictive, but it actually is for your protection as a young lady growing into a Queen—

protection for your throne, your respect, your body, and, last but not least, your reputation.

PRAYER

Father, in the name of Jesus, thank you so much for teaching me what modesty means. I want to be a godly example wherever I go. Help me to remain ladylike at all times and put a check in my spirit when I look in the mirror. Help me watch my mouth and create in me a clean heart so I can put away filthy and foul language and behavior no matter what I see and hear. Help my social media page to be a light to the world and encourage others to live righteously. Amen.

NOURISHMENT

So whether you eat or drink or whatever you do, do it all for the glory of God. (1 Corinthians 10:31)

ourishment is important at your age because the Bible says your body is a temple. You only get one body, and the choices you make now will determine your future health. God created you for a special purpose, and the last thing you want is to cut your life short because of the things you did when you were young. I started eating healthy around 19 years old. I used to eat everything in sight and thought as long as I stayed small, I was healthy, but that wasn't true. Food contains so many unhealthy things these days, so you have to be careful about what you eat and even the products you use. What we put in our bodies can either create an acidic space, where disease can settle in and grow, or we can eat to keep our bodies in an alkaline state so that disease doesn't have a chance to grow.

You have one body. Yes, you live under God's protection, but you have to use wisdom. You cannot expect to eat everything in sight, drink beer and alcohol seven days a week, smoke weed or cigarettes all day long, sit around drinking soda, eating candy, and only getting three hours of sleep at night and think you will have the energy and life you want. No, ma'am! Queens don't do any of that stuff because they have to be strong, sober, and healthy to fulfill their purpose and help others. We want to avoid diseases such as high blood pressure, diabetes, high cholesterol, cancer, fibroid tumors, and the list goes on and on. Just because your grandparents, parents, or aunts and uncles had a disease does not mean you have to deal with one. You can break that curse by making healthier choices.

EATING

You should eat between 1300 and 2000 calories a day depending on your height and weight. You can look it up or ask your doctor. Eat three meals a day with fresh fruits and vegetables, healthy proteins, less processed foods, and healthy snacks. I know some of you have to eat what your parents fix, or you are in college so it is hard to eat healthy; however, you can still build a healthy meal with what is in your refrigerator. Here are some tips I've used and still do even when I have to travel:

♛ Make half your plate fruits and vegetables. Choose red vegetables like tomatoes, orange vegetables like sweet potatoes, and dark green vegetables like kale and Brussel sprouts. One thing I noticed about eating broccoli (which everyone seems to love) is that it bloats you, so if you have an event that you have to be snatched for in a certain dress or pair of pants, avoid it so your stomach won't stick out too much. You should eat at least five to seven fruits and vegetables a day.

👑 I haven't had pork or beef in over 20 years. It always made me feel heavy and sluggish. It is also full of saturated fat, which isn't good for your heart. I eat fresh fish like trout and wild salmon most of the time. If you want to eat chicken and turkey, make sure it is organic so you can avoid eating pesticides and preservatives that aren't good for you. Trim the fat off all meat and limit your meat intake to 3 ounces, which is the size of a deck of cards, like half a skinless chicken breast or one skinless leg with the thigh.

👑 Include whole grains like oatmeal, brown rice, quinoa, couscous, and whole corn in your diet.

👑 Try to avoid extra fatty stuff like gravy and sauces. If you are like me, you probably like soul food like macaroni and cheese, sweet potato casseroles, cobblers, cakes, and pies. You can eat these things in moderation, but it shouldn't be Thanksgiving every week. I reward myself with foods like this when I accomplish one of my goals. If I get a new contract for my company or put on an amazing event after weeks or months of work, I cook or go to one of my favorite soul food restaurants and eat up everything. Then I go work those calories off and do a detox and feel better about being a greedy girl.

👑 I avoid fast food like the plague. I haven't pulled up at a drive-thru in more than 10 years. It's full of a lot of processed junk you don't want, hurts your stomach, and is bad for your skin and health. I know it is fast, cheap, and easy but you can make a healthy meal these days for the same price that will last you a few days.

👑 Limit the amount of fried foods you eat. Instead of frying chicken, bake or grill it.

👑 Watch your sugar and dessert intake. Right now, your metabolism is fast. Whatever you eat burns off quickly, and you may not see the effects of what you choose right away. Believe me, you will get to an age where everything ends up turning into fat on the gut, thighs, and butt and you'll wish you declined cakes, pies, and ice cream. I know it tastes good and you don't see any harm in dessert after dinner right now. Give yourself a cheat day. Instead of eating traditional desserts, replace them with fruit salad or even baked apples with cinnamon.

If you are already having issues with your weight or have been diagnosed with diabetes or a health issue, avoid or limit the following foods:

👑 **Sodas, sports drinks, and punch**. They are full of sugar and empty calories and have no nutrients. Replace them with water. If you need something bubbly, try sugar-free sparkling water. They have flavored water that helps me feel like I'm drinking soda. The more water you drink, the more you will have a thirst for it. You should drink half your body weight in ounces. If you weigh 125 lbs., you should drink at least 62.5 ounces of water. That is almost a gallon. It is a lot of water, and yes, you will want to run to the bathroom every five minutes at first, but your body will get used to it and you will be able to tell the difference in your skin, hair, and energy.

👑 **Processed lunch meat** has a lot of sodium. I know it is convenient, but making turkey or chicken parts and slicing it for your sandwich is much better for you. Go to the deli if you cannot cook and they will slice it from a turkey or chicken. It is better than the packaged meat.

👑 **Hot dogs and sausage.** I used to love hot dogs. I remember when someone told me how unhealthy they were for me, I hid them in the bottom of the fridge so they wouldn't see I still ate them. When I did my own research, I found that they have a lot of sodium and fat, and I didn't want any of the cholesterol or high blood pressure issues I had seen in my family. I finally threw them away once and for all.

👑 **Whole milk.** Yes, milk does a body good, but look for lower-fat options that won't make you gain weight. I drink almond milk.

👑 **Ice cream** is so good and is always a comfort when you're feeling down, but there are healthier versions that taste just as good. One brand I buy is called Halo. It is lower in sugar and calories and has all the good flavors. Try it and thank me later.

👑 **Creamy salad dressing** like blue cheese or ranch. Yes, it tastes good with chicken wings, but look for the light version so you won't add too many calories to your daily intake. All of that equals extra pounds.

👑 **Stick butter** should be replaced with olive oil or canola oil. Its lower in saturated fat and better for your heart.

👑 **Frozen french fries** are one of the most sodium-filled foods. YouTube how to take fresh red or sweet potatoes and cut them into strips and bake them in the oven with olive oil.

Healthy snacks include mixed nuts, Greek yogurt with mixed berries, apple slices with peanut butter (if you have acne, steer clear of peanut butter. Almond butter is a better alternative), celery sticks with cream cheese, kale chips, hard-boiled eggs, homemade trail mix (store-bought is too full of sugar), dark chocolate and almonds, carrots with blue cheese, and protein shakes.

DRINK WATER CHALLENGE

I told you how bad soda and sugary drinks are for you. Challenge yourself to drink more water every day until you reach your goal of half your body weight in ounces. Alkaline water is the best. That means the pH level is above 7. This will help flush out any toxins in your system, give you energy, clear your skin, grow your hair and nails, and, my personal favorite, flatten your belly! Once you get to your goal amount of water, try to drink that amount for 30 days straight with no juice, coffee, tea, sports drinks, soda, or punch. Document the changes you see and feel in your body. After the challenge, continue to drink more water than any other beverage.

If you don't like the taste of water, try infusing it with cut-up fruit. Simply wash the fruit, cut it into small pieces and add it to the water. Leave it in the refrigerator at least two to four hours OR leave it in overnight. A few of my favorite combinations are:

- Strawberry, lemon, and mint
- Watermelon, kiwi, and lime
- Mango, pineapple, and strawberry
- Orange, cranberry, and lime
- Cucumber, lemon, and mint

👑 Grapefruit, strawberry, and mint

👑 Strawberry, cucumber, and mint

EXERCISE

You knew this was coming, and if you're anything like me, you dread the thought of working out. I do it anyway for my health and to work off the snacks I like to eat. Some of you are athletes and get plenty of activity. Some of you will find any excuse not to leave the sofa or the bed. No matter how you feel about exercise, you have to get moving. Start with walking, do a 30-day squat challenge, jump rope, go for a run, download an app that will guide you through a workout, take a swim or Zumba class, join a gym, or even ask one of your more athletic friends to give you some pointers or work out with you. You can do some fun things like hiking a mountain while listening to music, taking up boxing or kickboxing, biking, or even joining a dance class.

Exercise builds muscle so you can be fit and not flabby and keeps your heart pumping, makes you stronger, and helps you live longer. You should exercise at least three days a week for at least half an hour, but doctors recommend an hour. Once you find what works for you, you'll enjoy doing it and it won't feel like such a drag. See your doctor before starting any workout.

After working out, you should eat a healthy meal with protein or drink a healthy whey protein shake. You can add berries, bananas, and even spinach to make a green smoothie, which tastes great and helps you get your five to seven servings of fruits and vegetables a day. Eating right and exercising will help you be more fit, strong, energized, and happy. Yes, happy! Exercising produces endorphins, which is a chemical that makes you feel positive. This will also help you think clearer and accomplish your goals.

Moderation is the key to life. I don't want you to feel you have to go to the extreme and ban yourself from eating some of the things you love, but I also don't want you to have the mindset I've seen in others that say, "Well, you gotta die of something" or "My great-grandpa smoked cigarettes and ate pork ribs every day and lived to be 92." Don't use these excuses to eat whatever, whenever and not take control of your health. God promises you a long life, but you have a responsibility to take care of the body He gave you.

PRAYER

Father, in the name of Jesus, your Word says that I am fearfully and wonderfully made. Thank you for giving me wisdom on how to eat right and take care of myself. Remind me to drink more water, exercise, and watch my sugar and fat intake. Free me from bad thinking about food and help me accept the body you gave me and work with it so I can live longer and feel as strong and as energized as possible to do your will. Amen.

OWNERSHIP

Whatever you find to do, do it well...
(Ecclesiastes 9:10a)

wnership is about taking responsibility and putting all your effort into it. When you take ownership, you are showing God that you are willing to take care of the things He's blessed you with. Growing up, I had the responsibility of going to school every day, keeping my mouth shut (which was the hardest thing for me because I love to talk), and doing my best to complete my classwork and homework. I loved school, so that came easy for me. I also had to pay attention in church on Sundays, learn songs for the choir, and remember Bible verses. I had no choice because we were in church for what seemed like 1,000 hours a week!

At home, I had to take baths or showers every day, brush and floss my teeth, separate my clothes for my mama to wash (we knew that we better not touch her washer and dryer!), and do my daily chores. This is where I fell short. I did NOT like washing dishes. In fact, I threw away dishes that were too hard to wash or pretended to forget to wash them. I still laugh at the memory of when my mama came into my room at night asking why the dishes weren't washed and I used cramps as my excuse.

Making my bed seemed like a waste of time back then. I was always rushing in the morning because I didn't listen when I was told to get things ready at night. Cleaning toilets was gross, and the only thing I liked to do was vacuum so I could see the pretty lines in the carpet, but of course, that was not enough to get out of the other chores. I had to take ownership for the things I was expected to do and realize that if I wanted to be a successful woman one day, I had to learn to do the things that would develop my discipline and sense of responsibility.

Jesus said: *"If you're honest in small things, you'll be honest in big things; If you're a crook in small things, you'll be a crook in big things. If you're not honest in small jobs, who will put you in charge of the store?"* (Luke 16:10-13)

Ownership is important because the habits you create now will shape you into who you are as a Queen. If you are junky growing up, you will likely be junky as an adult. If you are lazy now, those habits will set in and you won't see a reason to switch up when you get older. Responsibility is not a punishment. It is actually a test to see if you can be trusted with more. Why would God bless you with your own business if you can't get to anything on time now? Why would he give you a beautiful home if you're going to let dishes and trash pile up and have roaches running around? If you can't take care of your cute little bag from Target, why do you think you deserve a Chanel bag? Ownership gives you an opportunity to earn more and show how grateful you are for what you currently have.

You may have to rearrange your priorities a little so you can get everything done, but it will make you a better person and prepare you to juggle more important tasks in the future. I know it sucks to clean up and do chores you don't like, but it is so necessary to develop the qualities of a Queen. Queens are never lazy or dirty or smelly. They are clean, organized, and well put together. People judge you on how you and your house look, so present yourself as royalty and that is how you will be treated. Taking ownership is about putting pride in whatever belongs to you, whether it is your education, spiritual journey, bedroom, car, or clothing. A little organization and planning will keep them in the best shape possible.

BEDROOM/DORM ROOM/HOME

Find things that make your bedroom, dorm, or home more comfortable and more beautiful. Dust and polish your furniture, keep your floors swept or vacuumed. Choose your favorite color comforter or bedspread, buy a colored light bulb to give your room a beautiful glow. I have pink light bulbs from Amazon in my bedroom. I feel like I'm in a Barbie dream house when I turn the lamps on. Don't allow clothes to pile up until you are so overwhelmed you say forget it and let them pile up even more. When you come home after a long day of classes or work, put those clothes in the hamper or the dry-cleaning bag instead of throwing them over the chair or leaving them on the floor. When they are freshly washed and dried, fold them, hang them, and put them away immediately.

Organize your closet by color so it looks pretty and tidy. Use sachets of fragrance so that your clothes smell great and your closet is fresh. Buy the same type and color hangers and hang everything facing the same way. Taking ownership of where you live will make you feel proud of how pretty your closet looks. It's not for everyone else to see, but for you to walk into and keep organized every day. Use scrap cardboard to separate your dresser drawers into compartments for your panties, bras, pajamas, and tank tops. That way you know where everything is and can just slide things in. If you have some extra money, you can buy the drawer compartments from the store.

When you use the shower or tub, clean it out right away. When you allow the soap to stay in there day after day, you end up with black scum that contains germs and fungi, and that is disgusting. You can use natural white vinegar with lemon to spray your shower and tub down every day and won't even have to scrub. It'll leave a fresh scent and be sparkling clean. When you brush your teeth, wipe the mirror down with a paper towel and alcohol to get the toothpaste splatter off, and do the same with the faucets. Use your cleaning mixture on the sink. It takes not even two to five minutes to do this every morning or evening. That way when it is time to do chores on Saturdays, you won't have to scrub or clean for hours and hours. For each room you clean, reward yourself by lighting a good smelling candle and spray extra strength Febreze on your bed sheets and comforter set. Speaking of bed sheets, they should be changed weekly if not twice a week.

Play music while you do your chores. Sing to God and thank Him for every item you have. So many girls have less than you or nothing at all. I've met the happiest girls in other countries who live in one-room huts, have only a few outfits, and own one pair of shoes. If they can take care of their homes and belongings, you can show your appreciation for what you have been blessed with by taking care of all of it.

SCHOOL

Taking ownership of your education means taking it seriously. If you plan to go to college, you need good grades. If you plan to start a company, you need to know how to balance the books, create invoices, and market your business. Yes, you can hire people, but you need to know certain things so people won't steal from you or ruin everything you have built.

Use a calendar or planner to write down all of your assignments and projects to stay organized. Don't wait until the last minute. Give yourself plenty of time to complete them. Write a list of what you need to complete the projects and assignments so you have enough time to get them. If you need something that you can't find, ask your teacher, parent, or guardian. In group assignments, don't let everyone else pull their weight while you sit there letting them get all the credit. I have been in this situation before where I felt like I and a few others did all the work. There was always one person who did almost nothing but sat there and smiled while the teacher handed out an A+. Don't be that group mate. Take ownership. God is watching, and everything should be done like we are doing it for him.

APPEARANCE

I take pride in my appearance because it is the first thing people notice when they meet me. People will look at you from head to toe and make an instant judgment about who you may be as a person. If you look like you don't care, they will believe you don't care. If you look like you are lazy, they'll think you are lazy and treat you accordingly. What do people think when they first meet you? You don't have to be rich or wear the most expensive clothes to make a good impression. All it takes is a little time and effort to put a complete look together. Since we covered hair, nails, and body in the hygiene chapter, here are some other Do's and Don'ts so you can look polished and put together at all times.

Do's

- 👑 Buy the right size of clothing. If it is too big or too small, you will look frumpy or uncomfortable.
- 👑 Clean and iron all of your clothing. Not just the front or part that will be seen.
- 👑 Wear shapewear that gives you a proper foundation under your clothing. This will prevent your undergarments from being seen or anything jiggling when you walk.
- 👑 Clean and polish your shoes. Don't leave the house with stains, scuffs, or mud on your soles. Make sure your shoelaces stay crisp and clean. Even if you've been working on a farm, have a separate pair of shoes for that.
- 👑 Learn what colors go well with your skin tone.
- 👑 Learn what clothing cuts go well with your body type.
- 👑 Stand up straight and smile when you walk in a room. A smile is your best accessory.
- 👑 Get your pants hemmed or use hem tape and iron the hem. It looks very frumpy when your pants drag on the floor, and the last thing you want is to trip and fall.

Don't

👑 Overdo it with accessories. You don't need to put on every bracelet, necklace, and ring you own. Less is more. A pair of studs or hoops are simple and chic.

👑 Wear shoes that you can't walk in. The last thing you want is to look like you're in pain or wobbling everywhere. Somebody may even think you are drunk.

👑 Walk hunched over, too fast, or too slow. Pretend there is a book on your head.

👑 Forget your belt. It will cinch in your waist and make your pants look better.

👑 Wear items with stains, rips, holes, or tears.

ENTRANCE/EXIT CRITERIA

One of my favorite clients and mentors taught me the importance of entrance and exit criteria. It has helped me in all of my endeavors since then. You start out with a list of what you WANT to do, which is the exit criteria, and then write a list of what it will take to get it DONE, which is the entrance criteria.

For example, you want to wash and dry your hair. Have you ever gotten to the sink or shower to wash your hair and then realized you didn't have everything you needed? As you grow and mature, you'll find yourself doing things even more important than this, but practicing the entrance/exit criteria from small things to large projects will save you a lot of headaches. Let's continue with the hair washing and drying example to show you how it works:

The exit criteria (what you want to happen) are:

👑 Clean and conditioned hair

👑 Free of tangles

👑 Smells good

👑 Shiny but not greasy

👑 Dried

👑 Moisturized

👑 Then you write your entrance criteria (everything you'll need to make that happen.)

👑 Shampoo

👑 Conditioner

👑 Leave-in conditioner

👑 Heat protectant

👑 Blow dryer

👑 Comb

👑 Brush

👑 Oil

When you complete your entrance and exit criteria, that is the first step to creating a plan. Doing this little assignment before taking on any project will help you obtain a successful outcome. When you have your list, gather the supplies you need. Once that's done, you can get started knowing that you are well prepared.

OTHER WAYS TO TAKE OWNERSHIP

There are several other ways to take ownership:

👑 Take on an internship, job, or volunteer work. Be on time, listen to your supervisor, be respectful, smile, and do things in excellence instead of rushing and doing it halfway.

👑 Help your siblings with their homework; show them how to organize as you have learned.

👑 Keep your car cleaned and vacuumed and smelling great.

👑 If you see trash in your community, home, church, or school, pick it up and set an example for others.

👑 In your spiritual walk, read, pray, study, and praise to be closer to God and become more like Him.

APOLOGIZING

An important way to show maturity and ownership is apologizing and admitting when you are wrong. If you have hurt someone's feelings, if you spoke out of turn, or if you have made a mistake at work or school, taking ownership for it will not only gain respect from others but show that you don't walk in pride. It will not kill you to do this. Life isn't always pretty, and you will make mistakes. Some of them will be simple mistakes like bumping into someone or spilling your drink on the floor, but sometimes it'll be because you did something without thinking and damaged someone's feelings and property.

Suppose you borrowed your friend's white dress and didn't read the instructions on how to care for it. You irresponsibly threw it in with the dark clothes and the colors ran on it and turned her beautiful white dress pink. Instead of making excuses or hiding the truth, be honest and admit what you did. Take ownership of your mistake by doing what you can to make it right. If your mama told you to take the chicken out the freezer, do it immediately so you won't forget. If you do forget, at least call her, admit it, and attempt to order or make dinner so she won't have to worry about it. A true princess can swallow her pride and admit when she's wrong. Don't try to get out of your responsibilities. Take ownership of them and realize that doing them will prepare you for the next level of life so you can mature into the Queen you were created to be.

PRAYER

Father, in the name of Jesus, thank you for not always giving me what I want but always meeting my needs so I can grow and mature into who you called me to be. I know now that taking ownership of my responsibilities will allow me to develop the skills I need to fulfill my purpose and that even though it can be uncomfortable, it will stretch me and make me better. Forgive me for the times I murmured and complained while cleaning, doing schoolwork, or helping others. Thank you for blessing me with the ability to do these things because I know others are not as fortunate. Amen.

PURPOSE

For I know the plans I have for you," declares the
Lord, "plans to prosper you and not to harm you,
plans to give you hope and a future."
(Jeremiah 29:11)

You've heard the word *purpose* several times in this book, and I guarantee it will be the most important aspect of your life. Purpose is defined as *"the reason for which something is done or created or for which something exists."* God doesn't do anything without a purpose. Before you were born, He knew what He wanted you to do on this earth, and it is directly connected to helping others. Of course, he wants you to have fun and enjoy life; however, it is very important to find out your purpose now and start living it. Trust me, there is nothing like finding and living in your purpose every day. It is satisfying, fulfilling, and rewarding. When you listen to your favorite song and sing out loud and dance to the beat, how does it feel? Are you free and happy and in the groove? That is how fulfilling your purpose every day feels, and it comes so naturally! Everything He assigns me to do, it takes a lot of hard work and consistency, but it is directly in line with my skills and abilities and I enjoy doing it.

You have already learned how to dream and make them come true with hard work and dedication. Your dreams and God's purposes for you should be in line with each other. Your purpose was perfectly planned by your Father in Heaven before your parents even met. I know that sounds heavy, but it is actually a beautiful example of how much He loves you and how much you mean to Him. If you have a pulse, you have a purpose, but it is up to you to find it and work every day to fulfill it.

A good man leaves an inheritance to his children's children. (Proverbs 13:22)

After a long life, when God finally calls you home, what legacy do you want to leave on this Earth? A legacy is something left behind that will live on even after you are long gone. I want my great-great-great-grandchildren to see the work I did on behalf of the Lord while I was here on Earth. I want millions of girls to continue to be blessed by the programs, events, books, and products God helps me create to help them walk, talk, and live like Queens. A legacy is not just about money or property. It can also be the way you lived for God and how you put your purpose first.

Write down what you want people to say about you and all that you did for God's glory. When your God-given purpose becomes more important than the temporary pleasures of this world, you can truly build a legacy that God and others will be proud of, not ashamed of. I know traveling and going to concerts is fun. I know you think driving in fancy cars and going on endless shopping sprees is what true living is all about. I love these activities and doing them sometimes is not the issue. It is when you make those things a priority over your purpose. The only legacy those who make that decision will leave on this Earth are ticket stubs, boarding passes, and last season's clothes and shoes. Only what you do for God will last forever. What are you putting before your God-given purpose? Make the switch today.

SEEK GOD FOR YOUR PURPOSE (FIND, FLOW, AND FULFILL)

Finding your purpose is so important, and I encourage you to go after it. There are several books on finding your purpose. I recommend *The Purpose Driven Life* by Rick Warren, which put me on the path to finding my purpose. Once I found out that I was called to mentor, teach, and assist young girls like you to become amazing women of purpose, my entire life changed. God moved me to a new city, had me cut off the dead weight in my life, and caused me to make decisions that only benefited the purpose He shaped me for. No longer did I have the desire to hang out late at night, get drunk or high, waste money on frivolous things, and do things that would cause me not to be a good example to girls like you. When you find your purpose, it will add meaning to your life. Every decision you make will be so that you can make God proud by impacting the people He called you to affect. That is how this book came about.

When you live without purpose, you may feel like you are making progress, whether it is by going to school or work, but you will notice something is missing. When you finally find it, you will have a reason to live and keep going even when things are rough. Make a decision today to ask God about your purpose and for guidance on how to reach it. Make it your life's goal to hear, "Well done thy good and faithful servant."

PRAYER

Father, in the name of Jesus, thank you for creating me for a special purpose. Right now I'm young, but I know that if I lean on and rely on your guidance, you will show me why I am here and who I am supposed to help in this journey called life. Show me the people who are in my life to assist me and help me know who isn't supposed to be around. Give me skills, wisdom, and experiences that will shape me for my purpose and the faith to work every day to fulfill it. Amen.

QUEEN

Has anyone ever told you that you're royalty? Your Father in Heaven is the King and you are His daughter—a princess growing into a Queen. A Queen is not one who gives orders to her little subjects and never does anything for herself. A Queen doesn't look down at others or think she knows it all. A Queen definitely doesn't complain or act out when things don't go her way. We've seen those types of Queens on movies, but that is not what God wants for you. The Queen of England reigns and rules an entire country, but you are still a Queen even though you don't have a country to rule. You have been crowned by God. Your decisions rule your life, and you reign with Him while walking through life.

My personal definition of a Queen is a woman who walks in purpose and love, holds herself to a higher standard, has a beautiful light that shines from the inside out, and is a blessing to those around her. Princesses do the same thing, but before you are fully mature, you are learning lessons along the way that will grow you into your Queenship. The lessons I've learned from the many Queens in my life have shown me how to walk every day.

QUEENS LEAD BY EXAMPLE

Queens lead by setting an example for others even if it isn't the popular thing to do. There will be times in your life when you have to make a decision to lead or follow. One day, you may be pressured to try drugs or alcohol, break the law, or do something else you know is wrong. As a princess who will one day become a Queen, you have to be firm when going against wrongdoing. You don't have to give a speech or even list the reasons why. "NO" is a complete sentence. Put a smile on your face and confidently say, "No, thanks, I don't drink" or "No, thanks, I'll pass" and walk away. Ignore them if they try to put you down or make you feel bad for turning down something that will threaten your destiny. They don't wake you up in the morning, and anyone who makes you feel bad about having standards is not a real friend.

The more you stand up for yourself and take leadership of your life, the more comfortable you will be doing so. If your group of friends starts bullying someone, it is your responsibility to tell them they are wrong. Leaders are never comfortable being a bystander when someone is being treated unfairly. That doesn't mean jump into a fight and get yourself hurt, but it does mean showing compassion, speaking up, and not joining in on bad behavior toward someone else. Leaders do what's right no matter the consequences. Even if the person isn't being physically attacked, teasing is bad too. Words are so powerful. You have the power to bless or curse someone with what you speak over them. Watch your mouth and inspire others to do the same.

Another way to be a leader is to look for ways to help others. If someone is less fortunate than you and you can meet a need, approach them with love and genuine concern and offer to help them. It could be something small like zipping someone's dress in the back or paying for someone who doesn't have enough money for lunch. You never know how much it will mean to someone when you take the time to offer help.

To get experience as a leader, join the Student Government Association or lead a fundraiser. You can also join the Girl Scouts or a church organization that teaches you discipline and strength. If you are in the Atlanta area, you can join my organization, The Propel Initiative. If you are shy and don't like a lot of attention, you can still be a leader. Listening to your teachers, following the rules, getting good grades, reaching your goals, and volunteering are all examples of being a leader. Others will be inspired by your accomplishments and will follow suit.

Queens don't just talk about being a leader, they walk it out. One thing I try to do is remember people's names when I meet them and pay attention when they talk to me. Leadership skills take time and effort but are worth it. It shows others that you can be trusted and respected. It will also help you be more confident and comfortable in any environment such as college, work, or running your own company. Choose to lead and not follow and you will never regret it.

> **Blessed is the woman, who listens to me, awake and ready for me each morning, alert and responsive as I start my day's work. When you find me, you find life, real life to say nothing of God's good pleasure. (Proverbs 8:34-35)**

QUEENS STAY STRONG AND POSITIVE

Imagine yourself with an invisible crown on your head at all times. If you look down, your crown could slip or fall off. Life is not going to be as sweet as a bowl of ice cream every day. Times get so hard sometimes that you may wonder if it will ever get better. The key to staying strong is to tap into the power that God gives you. This must be done daily. Think of each day like a bank. You have to make deposits in order to make withdrawals. Spending time with the Lord praying, studying His Word, and writing down the plans He puts in your heart are all positive deposits you can make each day. You'll be able to withdraw strength, joy, faith, and so much more. Those things will give you the victory over any problem that comes your way so you can hold your head up high without worry even when you feel like you could scream.

We are told in Philippians 4:8, *"By filling your minds and meditating on things true, noble, reputable, authentic, compelling, gracious—the best, not the worst; the beautiful, not the ugly; things to praise, not things to curse."* To meditate is to think deeply about. Queens learn to train their brains to push past the noise of negativity by choosing to practice positivity. This type of attitude is contagious and will inspire everyone around you to do the same.

> *For You formed my inward parts; You covered me in my mother's womb. I will praise you, for I am fearfully and wonderfully made; marvelous are your works, and that my soul knows very well. (Psalm 139:13-14)*

QUEENS KNOW THEIR WORTH

God loves you so much! I don't even have enough words to tell you how much you mean to Him. Out of everything He created: the sun, the moon, the stars, the oceans, the mountains, and even the planets and all the different species of animals, you mean more to Him than anything! Say that out loud right now and as many times as it takes until you believe it: *I mean more to God than anything. I am worthy and valuable to Him. God loves me!* You don't need to make a million dollars, win an Oscar or Grammy, dress in designer clothes, or have perfect skin, a perfect shape, and long hair down to the floor to be valuable to Him. Of course, all of those things would be nice, but God saw you as priceless before you were even born and thinks you are amazing even with all your flaws.

God wants the best for you in every area of your life. When you know your worth, you don't lower your value for anyone! Just like Chanel and Louis Vuitton never have sales, you should never put yourself on discount. This means you should NEVER accept treatment that is less than a Queen deserves. Walk away from anyone who doesn't know your worth, and don't ever beg or try to convince them who you are. If they don't recognize it for themselves, it is their loss and their problem. Some people will try to test you, manipulate you, or trick you into ac-

cepting less just to see how pressed and desperate you are for their attention or validation. But you don't need that from them or anyone on this
planet. You have God's eye on you, and His validation is the only one
you'll ever need! I promise if you stick to your standards, the crazies, us-
ers, and clowns won't even have a chance to invade your life. Don't get
me wrong—they will try, but the minute you see signs that someone is
trying to pull you down and get you to cross a line, speak up and cut
them off if necessary. Never forget who you are to God and how important you are to advancing His Kingdom.

> **Take delight in the Lord, and he will give you the**
> **desires of your heart. Commit your way to the Lord;**
> **trust in him and he will do this. (Psalms 37:4-5)**

For example, if a guy is interested in you and asks for money or
gifts, say no. I've made this mistake before, thinking I was being ride or
die, but I was being dumb and dumber. If they call you out your name
like somebody off the street, don't answer. I met a guy who kept calling
me Ma. That was not cute to me, so I had to tell him, "Please don't call
me Ma . . . I am a Queen and my name is Tiffany. You don't know me
well enough to give me a nickname, so please don't call me that again."
Of course, he probably thought I was being uptight or too serious, but I
didn't care. Teach people what you accept, or they'll teach you what to
expect. If he tells you he has a girlfriend but wants to date you too, de-
cline. I don't care if he says they don't get along or she gets on his
nerves—don't believe it. Queens aren't side pieces. If he is expecting
wife treatment like sex, frequent meals, doing his laundry, or doing his

homework, cut him off. He is trying to get over and doesn't see you as a Queen. He sees you as something to play with. Queens are not toys.

Queens wait for kings. A king will prove that he knows your worth by honoring you and who you are. A king will go out of his way to do things that show he is serious about you. A king will not expect sex in return for a dinner or movie date. A king will invest time and effort into showing you that you are special. A king knows God, himself, and his purpose. If you meet a guy who doesn't know his purpose, he will be walking around lost and confused doing his own thing. That should be one of the first things you ask a guy. And if he's not following God, he can't lead you. Leave him alone and move on. A king will pray with you and for you, push you to greatness, and boost you up—not let you down. Allow God to send you the king He has in mind for you. Queens know their worth and refuse to settle.

PRAYER

Father, in the name of Jesus, thank you for fearfully and wonderfully creating me. I love that I am the apple of your eye and I have worth in you. Remind me to always walk, talk, live, and act as a princess who is maturing into a Queen. Expose, remove, and reveal the people who don't recognize my value and help me make the best decisions to lead, inspire, motivate, and stay positive as a Queen would. I love you, and I'm so grateful for your love and faithfulness toward me. Amen.

RESPECT

The second is this: 'You shall love your neighbor as yourself.' There is no other commandment greater than these. (Mark 12:31)

We hear the word respect all the time. "Respect your elders." "Respect your parents!" "Respect your teachers!" Respect starts with yourself. You can't respect others or even know how to receive respect from them if you don't first have self-respect. Self-respect is treating yourself with dignity and worth. When you respect yourself, you defend yourself against mistreatment and abuse and demand that others treat you with respect.

For everyone has sinned; we all fall short of God's glorious standard. Yet God, in His grace, freely makes us right in his sight. He did this through Christ Jesus when he freed us from the penalty for our sins. (Romans 3:23-24)

ACCEPT YOURSELF

So you made a mistake and popped off on somebody? Or you stole that money when no one was looking? Or you did the opposite of what your parents told you to do? I get it. Everyone makes mistakes. God still loves you and labels you **NOT GUILTY** because of Jesus' sacrifice of His life for you. Now it is time to forgive yourself. You can learn from your mistakes and ask God to help you make better decisions next time. Don't allow the past to make you change your level of respect for yourself. When you do that, the guilt will eat away at you, and when someone treats you with disrespect, you may think you deserve it.

I know sometimes you don't feel like you are enough, but the sooner you believe every day that you are, the smoother your life will be. The choices you make will show everyone the level of respect and love you have for yourself. If you believe you are enough, you will treat yourself with respect. The first step is to accept yourself—flaws and all. Instead of saying, "If I had straighter hair or if my skin was clearer, I'd be awesome!" No, that's not cool. You're awesome NOW, and nothing will make you more awesome than you already are.

If you don't feel confident and love yourself from head to toe right now, you will have an issue standing up for yourself when someone tries to disrespect you. Stop talking down on yourself and start complimenting yourself every day—several times if that is what it takes. When someone compliments you, believe and accept it and say thank you. The sooner you feel like you deserve love and respect, no matter how many flaws you *think* you have, the sooner you will start walking with your head up and not down. This will put you on the right track to respecting others and making sure they respect you in return.

BOUNDARIES

When you respect yourself, you set rules that protect you and your worth. There are certain lines you will not cross. When you refuse to have sex with a man who hasn't claimed you as his wife, you are showing respect for your purity. When you refuse to abuse alcohol and use drugs, eat right, and exercise, you are showing how much you respect your health and your body. When you walk with integrity and choose not to cheat, steal, or lie to get ahead, it isn't because you are afraid of getting caught but that you respect yourself too much to do anything that will lower your value. When you don't allow anyone to talk to you any kind of way, you are showing self-respect.

On that note, I want you to make sure you never put up with abuse of any kind. You either train someone to respect you (sometimes by walking away forever) or you'll be trained to accept disrespect. When someone knows they can get away with mistreating you or putting you down, you are showing how little respect you have for yourself. I call those people emotional vampires. They literally suck the life out of you. The longer you open yourself up to disrespect of any kind, the more damage you will be doing to yourself, your happiness, and your peace. Abuse can take from several months to several years to recover from. Immediately end all contact with anyone who puts you down.

When I was younger, I felt trapped in an abusive relationship. When I first met this guy, we were just friends. We hung out, talked on the phone, and I liked the attention he gave me. He told me I was gorgeous. After about a month, he started making comments about my personality, saying I was "prissy" and "girly." I never knew that was negative, but he said the words like he was saying "stinky" and "ugly." At first, I told him that is just the way I am, and he seemed to accept it. In between nice dates and long talks, he would complain about any and everything I did and made me feel like I was stupid. My lack of respect for myself fell for his apologies and attempts to buy my forgiveness with gifts and money. I thought, "He wouldn't continue to call me and do things for me if he didn't love me," but the truth was he didn't even love himself. His childhood was rough and his own self-image was damaged, so he had no idea how to love me like I deserved. When the abuse escalated from put-downs to violent outbursts, I knew I had to get away. It took me a few times to make it permanent but, looking back, I know it was because I didn't have enough respect for myself.

RESPECT FOR OTHERS

Now that you know how to respect yourself, you should know that respecting others is just as important. This respect not only includes those in authority over you like the police, your teachers, and your parents or guardians but also friends, neighbors, and strangers. Respect is honoring someone through your words and actions. This means you should listen to them without interruption, respond with an even tone of voice, and refrain from yelling at them and calling them names. Being polite shows respect. You should say "yes, ma'am" and "no, ma'am" to the elderly and those in authority over you. Saying "thank you" and "you're welcome" also shows respect. Think of some other ways you can show respect to the different people in your life. When you show respect, you get respect back.

PRAYER

Father, in the name of Jesus, thank you for teaching me how to respect myself and others. Help me to put that at the forefront of my mind when I interact with others. More importantly, help me to always respect my relationship with you. I want to live according to your Word and respect the body, life, and opportunities you give me. Help me learn to be a good listener and respect other people's opinions even when they aren't the same as mine. May the respect I show to myself, others, and You be an example of your love. Amen!

SUCCESS

Commit to the Lord whatever you do, and your plans will succeed. (Proverbs 16:3)

J love to cook, and my favorite thing to cook is soul food. I love jerk salmon, macaroni and cheese, angel eggs, collard greens, sweet potato casserole, and my favorite dessert—caramel cake. Every day would be Thanksgiving if I could get away with eating that kind of food all year long. Every good cook knows that no matter how good the recipe, you need the right ingredients so it will come out good.

This Book of the Law shall not depart from your mouth, but you shall meditate in it day and night, that you may observe to do according to all that is written in it. For then you will make your way prosperous, and then you will have good success. (Joshua 1:8)

You have to do the same thing to have good success. There are certain things you have to do **DO** to make your way **PROSPEROUS** and have **GOOD SUCCESS**. The Bible calls it GOOD success because there is such a thing as bad success. Some people seem to have it all, but they are stressed out, jealous-hearted, and angry. They may have money, cars, and a nice place to stay, but without God, there is no such thing as good success. I've created a recipe for good success so you can follow it and achieve the kind of success God loves and that you can be proud of.

GOD

The #1 ingredient, of course, is God. He created you, knows you better than anyone, and is the source of everything. Without Him, nothing is possible, so seeking His instructions is the key to making this recipe for success work. I can't tell you how important it is to make God the center of your life. Ask Him about any and everything and He will guide you.

FOCUS

Once you know your purpose and the instructions to follow, you need to stay focused. Think of a sharp point on a needle. Think of touching that point with your finger. Ouch! Yes, that is how sharp your focus must be to complete the major tasks it will take to succeed. You have to pull from something deep down inside of you to drown out any distractions to reach your goal. Set a deadline and make it happen. Sometimes, you'll have to miss the fun, hours of sleep, and time out with friends, but it will be worth it. None of those things matter when you are working toward something that will change your entire life. Every successful person will tell you that even though they didn't have all of the answers, their focus got them where they are.

SENSE OF HUMOR

On the road to good success, there will be bumps, twists, and turns. Instead of crashing and burning, sometimes you just have to laugh it off. I've planned so many events over the years, and right before it all falls into place, things go crazy. You have a choice to either let it bother you and make you quit or laugh, pray, and keep it moving. Things always work out in the end.

DILIGENCE

Committing to do the right things repeatedly is important. Don't stop until you're finished, and don't let anyone or anything discourage you. Even when you can't see the light at the end of the tunnel, keep going.

WORK ETHIC

Proverbs 23:33-34 says, *"A nap here, a nap there, a day off here, a day off there, sit back, take it easy—do you know what comes next? Just this: You can look forward to a dirt-poor life, with poverty as your permanent houseguest!"* A good work ethic is necessary for success. Laziness is unacceptable. Lateness is unacceptable. Doing things halfway is unacceptable. All those things lead to being broke and eliminating your chances for success. Step your game up and do more than is asked of you at all times.

Surely, Lord, you bless the righteous; you surround them with your favor as with a shield. (Psalms 5:12-13)

SECRET SAUCE: FAVOR

Have you ever had a teacher, classmate, or anyone else give you the hookup and you haven't done anything to get it? Has someone who acted a certain way toward you suddenly started being nice? That is called favor—that secret ingredient that only the children of God have access to. It will help you on your journey to success. When you fill out an application, start a business, or try to do something that you might need special treatment to get, pray and thank God for the favor that is always with you.

The journey to success is not an easy one. It also takes hard work, dedication, and passion. It will also take something that gives your recipe special flavor—your seasoning. My seasoning mix is creativity and organization. What's yours?

PRAYER

Father, I thank you that while I strive for good success, you are my boss and my co-worker and that I am never alone. Add your anointing and blessing to my recipe and give me the wisdom to follow your instructions and the strength to keep going even when it's hard. Help me succeed in everything I do, whether it's school, work, or my purpose. Serving you is my heart's desire, and everything I do will be done in excellence. Sharpen my focus and increase my faith to be able to accomplish your will for my life. Thank you for the people you will send my way who will give me favor and assistance while I'm headed to good success in Jesus' name. Amen.

T I M E

Help us to remember that our days are numbered, and help us to interpret our lives correctly. Set your wisdom deeply in our hearts so that we may accept your correction. (Psalms 90:12)

Have you ever heard the saying time is money? I believe time is worth more than money because you can never get it back. Once it's gone, it's gone forever. That is why it is important not to waste it. Right now, I know you have a lot of distractions that seem harmless, but when you want to be a Queen, your priorities should be in the proper order.

PRIORITIES

Priorities are about what is most important to you. What would you do anything to see happen in your life? What tasks would you put before anything? One of my mentees in Chicago is 15 and has a t-shirt line.

Ever since I met her four years ago, she has been super focused on her goals. Yes, she has fun spending time with friends and still Snapchats a few times a day, but she spends most of her time doing the things that matter so she can do the things she's dreamed of doing her whole life. Instead of calling me asking how to get a boy to notice her, she asks me how to expand her brand. Close your eyes and think of the things that matter to you most. Is it good grades? Time with family? Running your own business? Saving for a car? Write these things down. Those are the things you should spend most of your time doing.

The first time I met another young lady in Atlanta at my Queen Connection workshops, she gave me her business card. She is 17 years old with a cleaning company and was professional and well-spoken. Becoming a businesswoman was so important to her that she got her priorities straight and didn't let anything distract her.

Therefore see that you walk carefully [living life with honor, purpose, and courage; shunning those who tolerate and enable evil], not as the unwise, but as wise [sensible, intelligent, discerning people], making the very most of your time [on earth, recognizing and taking advantage of each opportunity and using it with wisdom and diligence], because the days are [filled with] evil. Therefore do not be foolish and thoughtless, but understand and firmly grasp what the will of the Lord is. (Ephesians 5:15-17)

TIME WASTERS

Time Wasters are activities that are fun but will take time away from your priorities. They seem harmless but can rob you of so much time that could be spent on making your dreams come true—for example, playing Candy Crush Saga and other pointless games on your phone, watching YouTube videos about somebody living in a van or eating crab legs, or scrolling through the ShadeRoom. These things pull you in so much that the activity you promised yourself would only take 5 minutes of your 24 hours, quickly turn into 1 to 2 hours a day. Multiply that by 365 days a year and you have spent a month on something that didn't make you money or make you better or bring you any closer to your goals.

Protect your time by replacing Time Wasters with activities that help you grow as a Queen. Instead of watching someone else on YouTube follow their dreams, watch something that will teach you how to follow yours. Instead of scrolling through the blogs laughing and commenting about celebrities who are making millions and living well, get rid of the things that are holding you back from doing the same for yourself. What are your time wasters? Is it social media? Is it television? How about talking on the phone with your friends? Write them down and reduce or eliminate the time you spend on them.

PROCRASTINATION

Putting things off until the last minute is like poison to your goals. Procrastination tells you, "I can do that later" or "I work better under pressure." I've used all of these excuses to avoid doing what I knew I had to do. If you wait until the last minute, you cannot get the same results you would if you took more time on the project. I used to wait until the last minute for my science fair project every year. My mama would be so frustrated because, of course, it was on her to find a subject and type what would go on my board, and my dad would have to do the project with me. Well, let's be honest. He basically did the whole project. It would have been easier and more fun if we started as soon as I got the assignment months before. Stop putting things off and just get them done. You'll be relieved when you complete the task you're putting off. The stress and anxiety from trying to rush will be gone, and you can use that time to do other important things.

TIPS FOR TIME

- 👑 Always be on time. When you have to be somewhere at 9:00 a.m., it is best to plan to get there 15 minutes early. Plan ahead for traffic or public transportation.

- 👑 At night, don't just pick out your outfit. Try it on so you can see if there are any snags, holes, wrinkles, or missing buttons. That way you can fix it, iron it, or choose something else. Don't forget your shoes and purse too. It doesn't make sense to get up, get dressed, and then realize that your black boots are lost.

- 👑 Pack your lunch at night if necessary.

- 👑 Go to bed early if you know you have to get up early.

- 👑 Use a planner to schedule each half hour. Start your mornings and end your day with God and then fill in other appointments, classes, and tasks.

- 👑 If an emergency comes up, call or text the person to let them know you will be late or can't make it.

👑 Prioritize your productive tasks first, then if you find yourself with an extra 15 minutes, choose to work or play.

👑 When you have an important new project or assignment, get up earlier. Waking up an hour early each day adds almost an extra full workday to your week. Millionaires wake up between 4 a.m. and 6 a.m.

👑 Take time for yourself. You deserve proper rest as well as time to eat and drink water and do fun things.

PRAYER

Father, in the name of Jesus, please show me how I use my time. Show me my time-wasting activities and help me prioritize what is important. Make me a wise time manager so I can choose the right tasks that will help me reach my goals. Lord, I surrender my time to you. Lead the way to the best things to do to make the most of each day. Give me the strength, energy, and courage to do it. Amen.

U N I Q U E

You saw me before I was born. Every day of my life was recorded in your book. Every moment was laid out before a single day had passed. (Psalms 139:16)

My favorite words to hear during wintertime as I was running around the house getting dressed for school was the weatherman's voice saying, "We are expecting a lot of snow this week." My sisters and I, my brother, and my favorite cousin would be so excited to wake up and see a bunch of snow piling up on the lawn, the cars, and the street and would go straight back to sleep to get some extra rest before going out to play in it. While my father was shoveling and we were sliding down the hill on trash can lids, I would think of what we were taught in science class—that no two snowflakes are alike. Now if God was creative and detailed enough to make snowflakes one of a kind, then He obviously put even more thought and creativity into making each person unique. God put a lot of thought into you even before you were in your mother's womb. There are seven billion people on the planet, and each one is one of a kind. Even twins who look just alike have differences that make them unlike anything else.

You should celebrate the fact that God put special qualities in you when He decided how you would look, talk, act, and move. The fact that your eyes are a certain color; that you are short, medium, or tall; that your mouth curves the way it does; and your voice sounds a certain way is not an accident or mistake. When you embrace the fact that nobody else is like you and never will be like you, you can become unstoppable. You'll stop trying to pose and dress like everyone else and start to find your own style. You may find out your humor makes you attractive. The way you think about the details may draw others to you. Your intelligence may get everyone's attention. Your skills on the swim or track team may be what sets you apart. Find what naturally makes you unique and nurture and celebrate it. When it feels natural and you don't feel like there is an off switch, you have found the key to what makes you special. Nobody is perfect, but everybody is special. God will work with you on the qualities that need to be improved and sharpened and make sure that what makes you unique will bless the right people.

> *Your hands made me and formed me; give me understanding to learn your commands. May those who fear you rejoice when they see me, for I have put my hope in your word. (Psalms 119:73-74)*

For instance, if you are very cheerful and have one of those laughs that make other people happy, someone may cross your path at school or work who is having a bad day. Your warm laughter and the light that shines from the inside out can change their view of the day. Someone could be planning suicide and just one cheerful smile and greeting from you can change their mind.

Being you is never a bad thing. Ask someone to describe your personality. Write that down and then list the things that make you special. Beside that list, write down how each quality can bless someone else. Yes, someone else may have a few of your qualities in common but the combination of your personality + your qualities + your special purpose = your God-given uniqueness. Embracing your uniqueness makes life worth living. Once you find this out, you find out your superpower.

PRAYER

Father, in the name of Jesus, thank you so much for making me your masterpiece! It is an honor to be one of a kind among the billions of people on this Earth. Help me embrace the way you made me from head to toe, inside and out, and celebrate my uniqueness. I know you do all things well, and I thank you for putting in me special qualities, talents, and traits that make me different from anyone else on the planet. I love you and ask that you continue to remind me of how excellent I am made, full of beauty and love for your ultimate glory! Amen.

VIRTUOUS

Do you not know that your bodies are temples of the Holy Spirit, who is in you, whom you have received from God? You are not your own
(1 Corinthians 6:19)

irtue is the quality of being pure. The best way to stay pure is to avoid premarital sex, masturbation, pornography, and oral sex. I won't list a bunch of Scriptures and tell you it is easy to wait for marriage to have sex. Premarital sex is everywhere you look—on commercials, television, and in books. It is at school, on campus, and even at church. Of course, I'll tell you what the Word says, but just telling you without explaining why may not work. That method didn't work for me. But I believe telling you the good, the bad, and the ugly about premarital sex will give you a clear picture of why staying pure is the best route to getting what you want, which is a lasting love that makes you feel secure, happy, cherished, respected, and free.

Premarital sex may feel good for a few minutes, but it comes with so many strings attached that are not worth the temporary pleasure. I was raised in the church and basically was told, "If you fornicate, you'll burn in hell" and "If you get pregnant and embarrass me at church, you'll put me in an early grave." Honestly, the church I grew up in did an awful job of teaching the importance of purity, self-worth, and God's love. All I heard was "DON'T DO THIS," but all I saw was "Oops! I did the opposite." So many people did any and everything that you couldn't even take what was being taught seriously. By the time I was 16, I was still a virgin, but most of my friends at church and school had already been having sex for years, and half of them had babies very young—I'm talking 13 and 15. I think I only waited out of fear of killing my grandmother. Since I didn't have a good understanding of how valuable I was to God back then, it didn't take much for my boyfriend at the time to talk me into finally having sex with him.

REASONS FOR REMAINING PURE

Following are some reasons for being virtuous and remaining pure:

Reason #1 – Secrets Come With Shame

When you have sex for the first time, it's painful and terrible. You just gave yourself away to someone just as easily as you would a bag of Doritos. Your innocence has disappeared. You feel mixed feelings right after, including shame, lust, anxiety, and loneliness. Shame because deep down, you know you have to hide it, and anything you have to creep and do is wrong. Lust because now you've opened the door to being aroused before you were meant to, and the devil can use that to tempt you to do it again and again. This is not love you're feeling. Love is patient. This is lust. Lust is impatient, never wants to wait, and doesn't care about the consequences. Anxiety comes because you are thinking 100 thoughts a minute and don't have a strong foundation for making sense of what you're feeling.

How can you be lonely after something that should bring you closer to someone? Because of the absence of love and the absence of God. Anything without God and love will leave an empty void the size of Texas that won't be filled with more premarital sex. My love for myself was non-existent, the connection I had to God was hanging by a thread, and the love I thought that boy had for me was based only on the physical. So I went home with no one to talk to about what I had done in the heat of the moment. I felt like the world was caving in. I had to keep it a secret from everyone. If you choose not to engage in premarital sex, you don't have to live in secret and shame.

I have heard of those mothers who give their daughters condoms and put them on birth control and tell them, "If you're going to do it, at least be safe," and you may have one of those moms. She is clearly thinking of your physical safety, but what about your emotional and spiritual safety? Those things are just as important. Giving yourself to a boy or a man who hasn't claimed you as his by marrying you puts you in a very dangerous place.

Reason #2 – Physical Danger

Sex is dangerous physically because of STDs. The nasty list includes:

- Gonorrhea, which can kill your chances of having a baby or can kill you if left untreated.
- Chlamydia can make you stink, give you belly pain, cause burning, and cause infertility.

👑 Hepatitis B can cause liver disease, and there is no cure.

👑 HPV can cause cancer and make you infertile, and there is no cure.

👑 Herpes has no cure and causes painful bumps. 1 in 6 people has it.

👑 Trich causes a foul odor and discharge.

👑 HIV/AIDS can kill you and has no cure. You have to take a lot of expensive meds. The long list of symptoms include fever, chills, muscle pain, a sore throat, and rashes, and those are just the mild symptoms.

Some of these guys don't take proper showers, and a musty dude doesn't even deserve to hold your hand. Other guys not only sleep around with several other girls, but they don't even use condoms. They may be walking around with untreated STDs. Those who seem clean, dress nice, and smell good may be gay. So many men are out here on the down-low sleeping with men and women.

Most guys treat sex as a game. Rapper Blueface has a song called "Thotiana," and he admitted in an interview that he slept with over 1,000 women in six months. Sleeping with somebody who thinks about sex so casually is like jumping in a pool of germs and filth! Some men are like pimps. They will lie to you, tell you they love you, and even pretend you are their one and only. Meanwhile, they are juggling several women and just looking for the desperate ones who will give them money, let them borrow their car, or help them with their homework. Believe me, it is just best to keep your legs closed. Your body is a gift, and the only one who has done anything to deserve it is Jesus. He died for you, and one way to honor Him is to stay pure. He meant for you to wait for marriage.

Reason #3 – Unplanned Pregnancy

According to the CDC, the United States has the highest rate of teen pregnancy in the world. Three in 10 girls get pregnant before age 20. That's nearly 750,000 teen pregnancies a year and almost 190,000 end in abortion. For the ones who had their babies, 8 out of 10 teen dads don't marry the mother of their child, half end up on welfare, more than half never graduate from high school, and only 2% graduate from college by 30.

When you have premarital sex, you not only open yourself up to STDs but you also risk getting pregnant at a very young age and delaying your plans for your life. Yes, babies are cute and cuddly, but they cost an average of $12,500 a year and take a lot of time and sacrifice. If you're determined, you can juggle the baby, the bills, the long work hours, and school, but if you have a choice, which would you choose—the struggle or the freedom? Most people I know don't regret their babies, but they regret the timing and wish they had waited.

Reason #4 – Guilt, Heartache, and Regrets

When it comes to abortion, the guilt that lies on your heart afterward is so heavy for cutting your baby's life short because of your own irresponsibility. It feels like a dresser full of bricks. If you let it, it will eat away at you for years like moths eat clothes. Trust me, I know the feeling. I had an abortion at 18 that totally rocked my world. A little over a year after I started having sex, my boyfriend had just left to go to college, and I found out on a Monday. I was so terrified of my friends, family, and church finding out that I set an appointment for six days later. I had a job and was in school and didn't want to take my life off track. I had to borrow half of the $400 it took to pay for it. I still remember the song playing while I heard something that sounded like a vacuum sucking the life I had made out of me as tears fell from my eyes. When I walked into the waiting room where my boyfriend waited, I tried to put on a brave face and act like I didn't care. I slept the rest of the day and by the next day, he drove back to school and I was left alone in Maryland to deal with the aftermath.

> *There is no fear in love. But perfect love drives out fear, because fear has to do with punishment. The one who fears is not made perfect in love. (1 John 4:18)*

If I had known about God's unfailing love for me, the fear of what people would think would not have caused me to make that regrettable decision. God is never surprised by your mistakes or choices. He created you and always knows what you will do before you do it. He promises to love you no matter what. If I trusted Him to take care of me back in 1998, I would have made a different decision. If you have already had an abortion or are pregnant now, trust that God has your back and, despite what you've done, He will forgive you and take care of you. The best way to avoid unplanned pregnancies, abortion, and guilt is not to have sex at all. It is not worth it.

Reason #5 – Nice Is Not Enough to Give Someone Your Body

You may think you're in love and that this guy is the one. I don't care if he buys you flowers every day or texts "I love you" every 10 minutes for a year straight. If he isn't leading you closer to God and is pressuring you to have sex, He isn't sent by God and you could end up broken-hearted. One thing I've learned is that **Nice is not and never will be enough**! The guy God has for you will offer more than a temporary feeling and good morning texts. He will wait for you, honor you with his last name by marrying you, and help you become the woman God created you to be. Don't fall for the tricks and traps Satan has laid in your path. The Bible warns us in 1 Peter 5:8 that Satan walks around **"as a roaring lion, seeking whom he may devour."** Don't set yourself up to be the prey. You are a Queen and deserve the best.

If a guy says he loves you, test his love by staying pure. If you have already given someone your virginity, ask God's forgiveness and start fresh. You must be different from the rest by knowing your worth and adding tax. Your body doesn't belong to any man who is not your husband. Make a promise to yourself and to God that you will wait for real love and marriage.

If you worked hard all week and went to cash your check and someone asked you for the cash in your wallet, would you give it away? So why would you lay down and give your body away so easily? God created you and you should honor Him by placing more value on yourself. Every time you have sex with someone you are not married to, you are creating and strengthening a soul tie. Those soul ties bond us to someone's mind, will, and emotions not just chemically but spiritually and emotionally as well. Even if they aren't good for you, you will find yourself so drawn to them that you will make excuses for their bad behavior, give them chances to continue to dishonor and disrespect you, and make poor decisions because of the soul tie and eventually become just like them. Sometimes their addictions become your addictions, their moods become your moods, and even their bad habits become your bad habits. Avoid this by avoiding sex outside of marriage.

Reason #6 – Soul Ties Are a Beast

If you think it is hard to abstain from sex, breaking a soul tie is even harder! It is like ripping a tree out of the ground with your bare hands. It is painful and difficult, and when you look back at the time you gave your most precious gift away to someone who did NOTHING to deserve it, you'll be upset. The word boyfriend or girlfriend isn't even in the Bible, so where did it come from? A girl and boy know nothing about life or relationships. To do things God's way, you want to meet someone at the right time, allow them to COURT you, and then have them MARRY you. It is meant to protect you from the things that will hurt you, distract you, and damage your well-being and self-esteem. The whole boyfriend/girlfriend thing is for kids—and kids play. Queen's don't.

How to Avoid Traps and Temptation

1 Corinthians 10:13 says that ***"God is faithful, who will not allow you to be tempted beyond what you are able, but with the temptation will also make the way of escape, that you may be able to bear it."*** This means that even when you're about to find yourself in a sticky situation, God will give you a way to say no, leave, or stop things in motion. If you aren't careful, it is easy to find yourself in situations that make you want to drop your panties. It is up to you to stay out of those or see them coming from a mile away.

Some common things guys will do to get you in one of these situations are:

👑 **Asking to cook you dinner for a first date.** Ask him to take you out for dinner instead and don't go to his house. Sex is not a reward for a date. If a guy wants to get to know you, he needs to ask you OUT, not in. If he can't spend a dime or make an effort to show he is interested, then he is not the one.

👑 **Asking to give you a massage.** Don't fall for this trap. Massage = sex. He'll start off at your neck and back and end up under your skirt.

👑 **Asking to cuddle.** Unmarried princesses and Queens should be in bed by themselves every night. The Bible says, "Stay away from the very appearance of evil." Plus, who will lay up next to somebody for long without trying something? Very few . . . stay away from the temptation.

You deserve more than a few moments of pleasure, a soul tie, and a broken heart. You deserve marriage, commitment, and real love. Don't play yourself and even entertain anything that gives you anything less. The Bible says in Romans 12:1 that the least you can do for all that God does for you is to *"present your bodies a living sacrifice, holy, acceptable unto God."*

PRAYER

Father, in the name of Jesus, thank you for loving me so much. I understand my value is worth more to you than rubies and that I was bought with a price. No man deserves me except my husband, so please kill my lust and fill me up with purity, righteousness, and your love so that I may respect my body and live a holy and pure life. I know that you created sex for married couples, so please give me the patience and strength to wait and hold my ground when I am pressured. Bless me with the gift of discernment so I can tell the difference from a man who is my purpose from one who is just my preference. I rebuke all counterfeits and thank you that you'll give me the wisdom to see them coming from a mile away. I will wait patiently for you to bless me with my husband and not fall into the traps Satan may set for me. Amen.

WISDOM

How much better is it to get wisdom than gold and to get understanding rather to be chosen than silver! (Proverbs 16:16)

When I think of wisdom, I think of someone who has lived a long life full of lessons, experience, and good juicy stories about their past. The truth is, not all old people are wise. Some of them never tapped into their God-given wisdom; however, you can live a life of wisdom starting now. Wisdom is different from education. Some of the wisest people I know don't have a college degree. Wisdom comes from God and is freely available to you like water. All you have to do is turn on the faucet and drink. The more you drink, the better you can live. It will grow every day if you let it.

~~~~~~

If any of you lacks wisdom, you should ask God, who gives generously to all without finding fault, and it will be given to you. (James 1:5)

~~~~~~

BENEFITS OF WISDOM

Think of a race when someone gives you a head start. This is what wisdom will do for you. While other people around you without wisdom are trying to tie their shoes, come up with a game plan, and figure out where the hurdles are, wisdom will show you the best way to get to the finish line without falling flat on your face. For example, wisdom will tell you how many college courses to sign up for because God already knows you'll be offered an internship that will give you college credit without taking an extra class. When you meet a new friend, wisdom will help you read between the lines of what the person is saying so you can see if their actions are genuine. Wisdom will tell you when to shut up before you go too far. Wisdom will not only help you get out of trouble that you got yourself into but help you avoid it the next time. It's safe to say we need wisdom.

~~~~~~

The wise woman builds her house, but with her own hands the foolish one tears hers down. (Proverbs 19:20)

~~~~~~

HOW TO GET IT

Wisdom can come from a few different places. The first source is experience. Say you trusted a friend with a secret and she opened her big mouth and told a bunch of people. Now your business is in the street. Wisdom will tell you not to tell her anything ever again and that she may not be as good a friend as you thought. Now you're faced with a choice. Apply the wisdom that you got from dealing with her before or trust her again and end up regretting it.

The second source of wisdom is through others. A wise teacher, mentor, or family member can guide you through a crisis or a situation. They may have been through what you are going through or they may be able to see the situation more clearly because their emotions aren't involved. For example, one of my friends was getting a divorce. She was struggling with deciding whether to take her daughter with her to another state or allow her to stay in Chicago with her school, church, family, and friends. She talked to her auntie who agreed that the best thing to do was to let her child finish the school year.

DIG DEEP

The Word of God is another great source of wisdom. It has so many great stories that will show when somebody had a hard choice to make and used wisdom to get through the messy parts of their life. For some real, practical wisdom that can help you in everyday life, start by reading one verse from the book of Proverbs a day and writing down what you learned from that verse.

The most important source of wisdom is God Himself. Since everyone comes from Him and He knows all things, it's best to have an open line of communication with him every single day, several times a day to get the inside scoop on whatever you're going through. He wants you to seek Him for everything—from small things about what to wear to an interview to make the best impression, what topic to write an essay on, or whether responding to the guy that keeps hitting you up in your DMs is a good idea.

Wisdom is the principal thing; therefore get wisdom: and with all thy getting get understanding. (Proverbs 4:7)

APPLYING WISDOM

Think before speaking and acting. Don't wait until your way fails. Go to God right away whenever you have a decision to make. Learn from the mistakes you made in the past and ask God to show you what you were supposed to learn from what you went through. I read something the other day that said, "I never lose. I either win or learn." Experience will help you grow in wisdom. Learn from other people's mistakes. If you see that someone blew all of their money shopping and now don't even have enough money to pay their cell phone bill, manage your money better so you don't go through the same thing. That is another way to apply wisdom. Help others. If someone is facing a decision and doesn't know what to do, pray with them and use wisdom to help them figure it out. Life won't always be smooth, but when you use wisdom, it makes things better.

Like clean water and healthy food, wisdom from God is one thing you can't live your best life without. It has nothing to do with what you learn in school or study in a book. You grow in wisdom through experience, lessons, spiritual knowledge, and prayer. Seeking wisdom from God shows that you don't know everything and have to rely on Him to make good decisions and live a good life. He wants what is best for you and has an open-door policy on wisdom, understanding, and guidance.

PRAYER

Father, in the name of Jesus, thank you for the gift of wisdom. I need your guidance every day to make my way smoother. Help me learn from my mistakes so I can do better next time. Bless me to help others with the wisdom that you give me. Give me the strength to apply the wisdom you have blessed me with and forgive me when I choose to do the wrong thing. I thank and praise you for your patience and mercy as I learn how to seek wisdom. Be strong when I am weak and make me wise. Amen.

X = UNKNOWN (FAITH)

And without faith it is impossible to please him, for whoever would draw near to God must believe that he exists and that he rewards those who seek him. (Hebrews 11:6)

Growing up, I couldn't stand math, especially algebra. All those X's on the page made me want to tear my eyes out. My hand would get weak and my armpits would get sweaty trying to figure out what the answers were. My mama got me a tutor in the 8th grade, but it still felt like I was reading a foreign language. I don't even know how I survived, and I'm so glad I never have to use algebra again. But guess what? There are still X's in my life because life has some unknown moments, but the best part about it is that God does the math for me as long as I have faith. There is a formula I use now to solve any unknown that comes my way:

Problem + Promise = Prayer x Faith + Action = Miracles

Faith is like having a flashlight in a dark room. It helps you keep moving even when you don't know where you're going and can't see that far ahead of you. It is like the gas in your car. It keeps the engine running so you can reach your destination. Faith is the key to pleasing God. I don't know about you, but I want to please God. When I learned this, I knew I had to learn what faith is and replace the X's with it. Let me show you how.

HOW TO REPLACE YOUR X'S WITH FAITH

Now faith is the assurance (title deed, confirmation) of things hoped for (divinely guaranteed), and the evidence of things not seen. (Hebrews 11:1)

Step 1: Turn His Promises Into Prayer

Faith is being 100% sure that you will receive what you prayed for. God's promises to you are in the Bible. Some of these promises include protection from harm, the supplies you need to live, peace, love, strength, wisdom, freedom, forgiveness, good health, and wealth, and that is only the beginning. God offers so many promises in the Bible that you can turn into a prayer. You can say, *"Father, in the name of Jesus, you promise in your Word to give me strength when I am weak. I need you to do that because I am going through something right now and need to be strong. Amen."* That is how prayer works. You turn God's promises into prayer. This is a lot easier than algebra.

Step #2: Add Faith

The next step is to believe and trust that God will come through with what He promised. Faith is like money. You can't go into the store and say *"Hey, I'm going to take this juice, pack of sunflower seeds, and gum . . . alright bye!"* and head out. Ummm, no. That's not how it works. You gotta have money, honey! Faith works the same way. You can't pray and then get up and say, *"Alright, Lord, gimme that"* and then complain, speak a bunch of negativities, cry, lie around, and doubt that what you prayed for will even happen." That is not faith. You must use faith to push what you prayed for into what you have.

When you buy frozen pizzas from the grocery store, the ingredients are solid and you can't eat it like that, so you have to put it in the oven. You preheat the oven to 475 and put the pizza on some foil so it won't drip cheese and smoke up the house. Then you set the timer and walk away, right? Does it ever cross your mind that the oven won't bake your pizza? Do you ever call your friend and say, *"Girl, I just put a pizza in the oven, and I do not think the cheese is gonna be melted all the way through . . . I just know that the crust is gonna be soggy and I'm not gonna have anything to eat! Girl, what am I gonna do? I am so hungry (cries) and this oven better work! I am super stressed cuz I had a taste for pizza today and I set the timer on 20 minutes, but the oven may not come through for me!"* No, you do not do that. You have faith that the oven will do what it is supposed to do and cook your pizza to cheesy perfection. Those toppings will be just right, and the crust will be amazing! If you have that much faith in an appliance, shouldn't you believe God will come through on His promises after you prayed?

Here are the top three things you must do after you pray:

1. **Speak the Word only!** If you don't know the Word, read it, listen to it, and learn it. You cannot speak the opposite of what you prayed. If you don't talk down on the oven, don't talk down on God. Watch your mouth!

2. **Thank and praise God!** Instead of praying the same prayer again, thank Him next time you pray. Say, "Thank you, Father, for blessing me with the strength to get through this situation. You are awesome and faithful." That shows you already believe it is yours!

3. **Claim it!** If people ask you about the situation, say, "God has already given me the strength to get through it . . . I got this!"

Truly, truly, I say to you, whatever you ask of the Father in my name, he will give it to you. (John 16:23)

Step #3: Patiently Wait

No matter what it looks like and how weak you may feel even after praying, trust that God will come through with strength right when you need it. Don't complain; don't cry. God will comfort you when you shed a tear, but faith is the only thing that will move God. Tears won't. If you believe what you prayed for is yours and don't speak against your prayer, you are using faith. God will be pleased with you when you do that and come through in the clutch.

Step #4: Celebrate and Keep Walking by Faith

God came through! You didn't doubt; you claimed it and praised Him, and He gave you the strength you needed to get through your hard time. Keep praising Him because He always hears your prayers and comes through for you.

Now is not the time to stop. The Bible says several times (James 1:17, Gal 3:11, Heb 10:38) that *"the just shall live by faith."* If you are a righteous believer in God, you do this every day. Every day takes faith. Faith that your transportation to school or work won't fail and you'll get there on time. Faith that you wake up with good health, in your right mind, and can move, breathe, swallow, dance, blink, and even digest your food. Faith that you'll be safe from hurt, harm, or danger. Faith that you have unlimited joy and peace and love in your life. You don't know how any of these things work, but you still believe that they will because *"we walk by faith and not by sight"* (*2 Corinthians* 5:7). You can't see it, but you believe it. What else are you believing God for? Write those things down and look up a Scripture in the Bible for them. Turn God's promises into prayers and continue to walk by faith.

Faith cometh by hearing, and hearing by the word of God (Romans 10:17)

Step #5 Grow Your Faith

Just like when you eat healthy food and it gives you strength, energy, and nutrition, hearing the Word gives you faith—faith in His promises, faith in miracles, faith in His love for you. It is important to hear the Word on a regular basis. You can listen to the Bible App, listen to your favorite preachers, attend youth and women's conferences, and go to Sunday service and Bible study. This will strengthen and build your faith to believe everything God promised can happen, whether you have bad news, an evil report from the doctor, or a major crisis.

~~~~~~

> ***As the body without the spirit is dead, so faith without works is dead. (James 2:26)***

~~~~~~

God wants you to live healthy, whole lives, and He cares about every part of your life, even the cares that seem small. If you are struggling with acne, your faith can clear it up. If you want to do better in your classes, your faith can strengthen your memory when it's test time. When you want to get along better with a family member, your faith can fix it. If you're sick, your faith can heal you. Give it to God; do your part by speaking the Word and working toward your goal, and your faith will get the job done. Dig deep in your Word, write down the promises you need God to fulfill, turn them into prayers, speak the Word only, get to work on your goals, and watch your faith pull them into your life.

PRAYER

Father, I come before you in the name of Jesus, and I choose to please you every day by walking by faith and not fear. I know that faith and fear cannot be in the same place, so I rebuke fear in Jesus' name! Show me the areas where fear tries to take control so I can replace it with faith. Your Word says I can build up my faith by reading and hearing your Word. I will study and seek your Word so that my faith can be strong enough to accomplish anything. Thank you that I can trust in you, your Word, your peace, and your safety. Thank you for surrounding me with angels to protect me everywhere I go. Amen!

YOU

And this same God who takes care of me will supply all your needs from his glorious riches, which have been given to us in Christ Jesus. (Philippians 4:19)

This book is to teach you how to apply the principles that will create a beautiful life and become a Queen. When you change your thoughts and mindset, you can change everything. The key to doing this is knowing who you are. Anytime you feel down or confused and need to know who you are and whose you are, read the following Scriptures and confessions and say them out loud, if necessary, to be reminded of your worth to God and your identity in Christ. God loves you so much, and once you start walking and talking like you know it, your life will change, your interactions with others will change, and you won't even give certain things attention or focus. You'll look at sin like it is covered in vomit and avoid it. You'll look at distractions as something that fell out of the trash in your path and step over them. Knowing your worth will keep you from settling and doing things that are beneath you. You won't let yourself lose focus and you will stay on the straight path to the success God has laid out for you in every area of your life. This doesn't mean you won't make mistakes, but you won't stay down. You'll dust yourself off and bounce back like never before.

Yet to all who did receive him, to those who believed in his name, he gave the right to become children of God (John 1:12).

👑 **YOU ARE HIS CHILD.** Even if you don't have parents or you feel alone, be encouraged knowing that your Heavenly Father wants the very best for you and has a perfect plan for your life that will give you everything you need and want to live it out.

So God created mankind in his own image, in the image of God he created them; male and female he created them (Genesis 1:27).

👑 **YOU ARE MADE IN HIS IMAGE.** When God created the world and everything in it, He did it by saying, "Be," and what He spoke came to life! He has given you the authority to do the same by commanding what you want to see like the Queen you are becoming. When you see something going wrong in your life, you can change it by commanding it to line up with the Word of God. Yes, you have the power to change your circumstances because God made you to be like Him through His Spirit! Believe it and use it and never let anything overtake you. You are valuable to God and are here to make a change when there is chaos and confusion with your words.

I am chosen by God, forgiven and justified through Christ. I have a compassionate heart, kindness, humility, meekness, and patience (Romans 8:33; Colossians 3:12).

👑 **YOU ARE CHOSEN BY GOD.** God chose you and put you at the top of the list of all of His creations. He has proven his love for you and will always be there for you. Instead of leaving you alone to walk around lost and in the dark, He created you for a purpose and to walk in the light.

I have the mind of Christ (1 Corinthians 2:16; Philippians 2:5).

👑 **YOU HAVE THE MIND OF CHRIST.** Depending on what is going on in your life, what you've seen or been through, sometimes scary, bad thoughts will come into your mind and try to make you believe them. You don't have to accept those thoughts. The mind of Christ is strong, sane, stable, and powerful. Take control of your thoughts and ask God to help you think like Him. Once your mind is set on higher things, you can do anything.

The Spirit of God, who is greater than the enemy in the world, lives in me (1 John 4:4).

👑 **GOD LIVES IN YOU.** God is powerful and has already defeated your enemies. You have nothing to fear. The same Spirit who conquered death lives in you. Receive that and know you can rely on God, who lives in you and works through you.

The Lord will make you the head, not the tail. If you pay attention to the commands of the Lord your God that I give you this day and carefully follow them, you will always be at the top, never at the bottom (Deuteronomy 28:13).

♚ **YOU ARE THE HEAD ONLY.** Even when life hands you a big blow, you will end up on top of your circumstances. My grandmother always said God sits high and looks low. He sees everything you're going through and will still cause you to win no matter what, even when it doesn't look like it. Say out loud every day, "I am the head only and never the tail," and you will see it.

I am redeemed—forgiven of all my sins and made clean—through the blood of Christ (Ephesians 1:7).

♚ **YOU ARE FORGIVEN.** Even when people keep track of the things you've done wrong, God will always forgive you. Before you even thought about sinning, Jesus died for your sins and took the punishment. Through His grace and blood, you are clean and forgiven forever.

I am redeemed from the curse of sin, sickness, and poverty (Galatians 3:13).

♚ **YOU ARE REDEEMED.** To be redeemed means to be bought back. People take things to the pawnshop when they need money. If they don't come back to pay for it before it gets sold, it's lost forever. Jesus paid for your life so you wouldn't be sold and gone forever. He bought you back and now you're free to live, love, and prosper.

I am healed and whole in Jesus (Isaiah 53:5; 1 Peter 2:24).

👑 **YOU ARE HEALED AND WHOLE.** When sickness tries to attack your body, command your body to line up with God's Word! You are healed by the scars that Jesus took on the cross. All you have to do is receive your healing. God wants you to have nothing missing, lacking, or broken in your body. Walk in your good health.

I am greatly loved by God (John 3:16; Ephesians 2:4; Colossians 3:12; 1 Thessalonians 1:4).

👑 **YOU ARE LOVED.** Sometimes you will feel you are all alone in the world. You'll cry so hard your head hurts, your nose will be stopped up, and your eyes will be swollen. Dry your tears, little sister. Your Father in Heaven loves you more than anything. He is right there waiting to hear from you. Pour out your heart to Him and allow Him to take the pain away.

I have everything I need to live a godly life and am equipped to live in His divine nature (2 Peter 1:3-4).

👑 **YOU ARE EQUIPPED.** When you know God for yourself, He will give you everything you need to live a great life and to follow His Word. All you have to do is open yourself up to His goodness.

I am a new creation in Christ (2 Corinthians 5:17).

👑 **YOU ARE A NEW CREATURE.** From the day you accept God, you are brand new. Forget about the past and never look back. God will change you from the inside out and give you a chance at a beautiful future.

PRAYER

Father, in the name of Jesus, if I had 10,000 tongues, I couldn't thank you enough for everything you've done for me. All the promises you've given me in your Word overwhelm me with gratitude and emotion. If it wasn't for you sending your Son Jesus to die for my sins, I would never be able to have a relationship with you that gives me everything I need in this crazy world. I give you all glory and honor for your faithfulness, your mercy, and your lovingkindness in my life. Amen!

Z E A L

But those who trust in the Lord for help will find their strength renewed. They will rise on wings like eagles; they will run and not get weary; they will walk and not grow weak. (Isaiah 40:31)

Have you ever been so excited and passionate about your goals when you start a new project, join an organization, or start a new job? Then a few issues came up and, suddenly, you lose the positive energy you had and quit before you even get a running start? I've been that way too—started something and never finished it. It just seemed like the excitement suddenly wore off. Life is like a race. You have to keep going until you finish. You can see it to the end with excitement without losing your breath and giving up. You just have to have zeal.

Life can be a rollercoaster. You get strapped into the ride and you're so full of nerves and excitement when you're going up the long hill before the big drop. You know it is coming, so you close your eyes and get ready for it to take your breath away while you try to scream. But as soon as the drop is over, the twists and turns begin and the ride is over, and you talk about how amazing it was. That is how life is. When you decide to live for God, obey His Word, and be an example in this world by working to fulfill your purpose, you should have a zeal that pushes you every day, even when something happens that makes your stomach drop and makes you lose your breath. The excitement for the ride of life should make you continue until the twists and turns are over. Everything you do should be met with excitement to see the things God has placed you here to do because you love Him and want to please Him.

Zeal is to have great energy or enthusiasm in pursuit of a cause or an objective. When you have a zeal for something, it means you go after it with passion. It is like a force that pushes you and drives you to greatness. Since life is not always easy, it is important that you don't allow anything to cause you to lose your zeal.

HOW TO AVOID LOSING YOUR ZEAL

Therefore, my beloved brethren, be steadfast, immovable, always abounding in the work of the Lord, knowing that your toil is not in vain in the Lord. (1 Corinthians 15:58)

There are several ways you can avoid losing your zeal.

MAKE SURE WHAT YOU'RE DOING IS YOUR PURPOSE

Your purpose lines up with your natural skills and talents. For example, you love doing hair and when people talk to you, they feel encouraged and loved because of your listening ear and warm heart. Your purpose may be to open a hair salon and encourage your clients. Some of them will be comfortable enough to talk to you about their issues, and just a kind word or quick prayer may change their perspective on their lives.

Write down the things that come easy to you, that you are good at, and that you are enthusiastic about and make sure they match what you are doing. If you know that is what you are called to do and are passionate about what God has put in your heart to accomplish, your zeal for Him will help you handle the obstacles with ease and go above and beyond to give the best service you can. Purpose and passion go hand in hand. You can't have one without the other. Find your purpose and your passion will flow out of you.

> ***Do not be deceived: "Bad company ruins good morals." (1 Corinthians 15:33)***

HANG AROUND OTHER ENTHUSIASTIC PEOPLE

There's a saying that you are like the five people you hang around most. Write down your five closest friends. Are those people focused on purpose? Are those people passionate and energetic about doing the things of God? Are those people going to great lengths to do something other than sit in their pajamas all the time binge-watching Netflix? Or are they so focused on doing hookah, partying, taking shots, and wasting time on things that don't matter? If the people close to you don't inspire you to stay passionate about what you are here to do, it may be time to rearrange your circle of friends.

~~~~~~

Love the Lord your God with all your heart and with all your soul and with all your mind. This is the first and greatest commandment. (Matthew 22:37)

~~~~~~

STAY CLOSE TO GOD

The reason you do anything should be because you love God and want to please Him. If you stay close to Him, you can never go wrong. A relationship with God is the most important one you'll ever have. Everything I do gives me so much joy because I know I was meant to do it and because He created me for it. That alone gives me the zeal I need to succeed and keep going no matter how hard and frustrating life gets.

Loving God means you will also love His people. Your purpose should directly help the people you encounter. Seeing the smiles on someone's face when I know the words I spoke or the events I planned or the work I did changed their lives in even a small way keep my zeal bank full and flowing.

PRAYER

Father, in the name of Jesus, I want to be excited about everything you have in store for me to do in this life. Help me to keep my spiritual zeal as I serve you and grow on this journey. I devote myself to you and want to do the right thing by loving you, your people, and serving them through the purpose you created me for. Help me bring honor to you and help me stay focused. Show me when the people around me are pulling me down and give me the wisdom to know how to handle it. Please keep me on the straight path forever and ever. Amen!

CONCLUSION

ecoming a Queen is not something you automatically become just because you put it in your social media profile, call yourself one, or because you wear a t-shirt that says it. It is so much deeper. Becoming a Queen will not happen just because you get older and people start referring to you as an adult. Yes, you will be able to remind some people that you're grown and can make your own decisions. Yes, you will have more responsibilities as you try to master the art of "adulting" by doing things like paying bills, getting your own place, getting married, having children, graduating from school, and starting a career. Those things don't make you a Queen. They make you an adult woman. I know a lot of adult women who are not walking in their Queendom because they have never been taught that they were born to be one and don't know where to start on becoming one.

Becoming a Queen isn't something that I did overnight, and I had a later start than you. I didn't realize who I was, what I was capable of, and why I was here until well into my 20s. Even then, it took time to allow God to heal the wounds that were created when I didn't know I was a Queen. It took time to recover from the bad choices I made when I thought I wasn't good enough. It took lots of prayer and many lessons to learn what I deserved so that I could immediately reject anything less than God's best for my life. Becoming a Queen is a lifelong journey, but it is so rewarding because instead of spending your time going around and around in a circle of confusion, shame, and pain, you will be able to avoid and ignore the things that are sent to knock off your crown.

The difference between being a woman and being a Queen is a Queen has taken the time, effort, and energy to develop herself with the help of God. A true Queen uses the years leading up to adulthood to learn and become grounded in her self-worth, discover and start to walk in her purpose, and gain wisdom in order to make healthy and productive decisions throughout her entire life. Applying the principles in this book will become a lifestyle that sticks with you and create an invisible crown of peace, love, and fulfillment.

Becoming a true Queen will show up in your actions, words, attitude, and the way you carry yourself. The minute someone meets you, sees your smile, and hears the confidence in your voice, they will see the light coming from inside of you and know you are a Queen without you ever having to use the word. People will treat you the way you deserve, and you will not entertain anyone who doesn't know better. This will also cause you to flow in the gifts God put inside of you so you can make your mark in the world. Everything you do will be done *on purpose*, and like a beautiful flower, you will bloom forever.

I will never tell you that life will be perfect on your path to becoming a Queen, but I will tell you that the sooner you realize who you are, the sooner you can create the meaningful, happy and whole life that you were born to have. Don't ever give up on yourself. No matter what it looks like, what you have experienced, or what you are going through even now, you deserve your crown. God loves you; I am praying for you, and you can become the Queen you were meant to be.

Made in the USA
Middletown, DE
29 November 2019